essential
cat

essential
cat

Caroline Davis

The Ultimate Guide to
Caring for Your Cat

Reader's
Digest

The Reader's Digest Association, Inc.
Pleasantville, NY/Montreal/Sydney

A READER'S DIGEST BOOK

This edition published by The Reader's Digest Association by arrangement with Hamlyn, a division of Octopus Publishing Group Ltd.

Copyright © 2005

FOR HAMLYN
Executive Editor: Trevor Davies
Executive Art Editor: Leigh Jones
Editor: Katy Denny
Designer: Jo Tapper
Picture Librarian: Jennifer Veall
Senior Picture Researcher: Christine Junemann
Senior Production Controller: Jo Sim
Index compiled by Indexing Specialists

FOR READER'S DIGEST
U.S. Project Editor: Jane Sherman
Canadian Project Editor: Pamela Johnson
Project Designer: George McKeon
Executive Editor, Trade Publishing: Dolores York
Director, Trade Publishing: Christopher T. Reggio
Vice President & Publisher, Trade Publishing: Harold Clarke

Library of Congress Cataloging in Publication Data
Davis, Caroline, 1971-
    Essential cat / Caroline Davis.
        p. cm.
ISBN# 0-7621-0496-1
    1. Cats. w. Cats—Health. I. Title.

SF447.D34 2005
636.8—dc22

2003060556

Address any comments about *Essential Cat* to:
        The Reader's Digest Association, Inc
        Adult Trade Publishing
        Reader's Digest Road
        Pleasantville, NY 10570-7000

For more Reader's Digest products and information, visit our website:
        www.rd.com (in the United States)
        www.readersdigest.ca (in Canada)

Printed in China

1 3 5 7 9 10 8 6 4 2

CONTENTS

INTRODUCTION

"A home without a cat, and a well-fed, well-petted and properly revered cat, may be a perfect home, perhaps, but how can it prove its title?" questioned the American author Mark Twain (1835–1910)—and he had a point. Somehow, as any cat lover will confirm, a cat does seem to make a home feel more welcoming, more friendly, and even safer and more secure. Even those who profess not to like cats tend to change their opinion once they get to know what makes cats tick. For those who adore felines in whatever shape or form they present themselves, life is simply not complete without a cat waiting at the door to greet them, sinuously weaving around their legs for attention, and, later, curling up, relaxed and purring, on their laps for a comforting mutual admiration session.

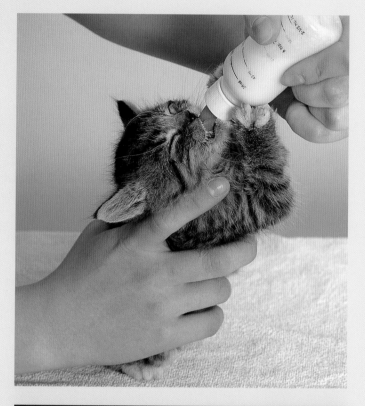

Why do cats make good pets?

In the United States and Canada (though not Australia), cats are now more popular than dogs. Perhaps the main reasons for this are their relative independence and ability to exercise and relieve themselves without human assistance, making them less trouble to own than dogs, who need companionship and someone to let them out regularly. As the checklist here shows, cats have several advantages over dogs.

Checklist

✓ independent
✓ self-exercising
✓ quiet
✓ clean
✓ inexpensive to maintain
✓ small
✓ playful

Companionship

A cat not only provides good company, he also imparts a sense of peace and tranquility in a chaotic, stressful world. Research has shown that having a cat—or any pet—can help us relax and recover from illness, as well as keep us alert and lively as we age.

Cats are naturally self-reliant animals, although we need to protect them in urban areas, where they are especially vulnerable to passing traffic. Cats are more independent by nature than dogs, but they can prove to be very loyal and rewarding companions and will ask for little in return except food, shelter, and affection.

Exercise

In general, cats exercise themselves through hunting (if allowed outside) and play. Some owners, whether they live in urban or rural areas, build enclosed runs in their yards so that their cats can have freedom and fresh air without risking their safety.

Daily care

In comparison with some other household pets, a cat's daily needs are relatively few, although longhaired breeds need daily brushing to prevent coat and skin problems. Cats are usually fastidious about grooming and washing themselves, so bathing is not normally necessary, but frequent brushing will help keep shed hair in the house to a minimum.

Cats make entertaining playmates for people of all ages. Not only will daily interactive play with your cat provide great entertainment for you both, it will also strengthen the bond between you, help keep the cat occupied (and less prone to behavior problems), and ensure he gets sufficient exercise.

With today's high standards in veterinary medicine and feline food, pet cats can live well into their teens—or even longer.

Frequently asked question

Q I am at work all day and am worried that a cat who is kept indoors all the time will get bored. How can I prevent this?

A One of the best ways would be to provide a companion pet. If this is another cat, you should ideally get two kittens to begin with so they will settle down and remain friendly, since an older and a younger cat may not get along too well. See page 21 for the pros and cons of getting one cat or two.

Maintenance costs

Cats are inexpensive to keep. Other than food and cat litter on a weekly basis, the only other regular expenses will be parasite treatments as recommended by a vet, annual vaccinations against the diseases cats are susceptible to, a veterinary health check every 12 months, and toys to play with (you will find that small scrunched-up balls of paper and Ping-Pong balls do the job admirably). Although an optional expense, pet insurance can be a wise investment; should your pet suffer an accident or illness, any necessary veterinary treatment could be very expensive.

Feline fact

The Egyptian word for cat is *mau*, which also means "to see," and it was linked to the concept of the eye of Ra and the eye of Horus—twin symbols of the sun and the moon. Some believe that the word *meow* derives from *mau*.

Advantages

Cats don't bark and howl, so your neighbors won't be upset on that score, which is especially important if you live in a highly populated, built-up area. As long as he is fed regularly; he has clean, fresh water available to drink; his litter box is kept clean; and he has a safe area in which to exercise and rest, plus some toys to play with, a cat will be content. If he is sociable and has a warm lap to sit on and a gentle hand to stroke him now and then, he will be a very happy cat, eager to reciprocate his owner's affection.

Type of accommodations

Cats can live quite happily in most homes. Many town and city dwellers keep their cats entirely indoors without any problems. In high-rise buildings, though, it's a good idea to put protective screens on windows and balconies to prevent cats from falling.

LEFT *Ensure that open upstairs windows are secured so your cat can't squeeze through them; better yet, fix mesh or wire safety screens to them so there's no risk of your cat falling.*

RIGHT *If you are often away from home for most of the day, getting two cats may be a good idea. They will keep each other company while you aren't there to give them attention.*

CHOOSING A CAT

Cats differ greatly in their needs, personalities, and ideal living situations, so it's important to choose a cat who will be happy to live with you and one you will be proud to own. Do you have time for the daily grooming needed by a longhaired cat? Do you want a sociable, affectionate cat or a more independent companion? Would a more mature cat be a more appropriate addition to your household than a kitten? Be sure to make an informed choice by reading the following pages carefully.

Cross-bred or pedigreed?

You may have an idea of your ideal cat in terms of color, type, and temperament—one who is pretty, is affectionate toward you, and behaves perfectly in all respects. However, you must bear in mind that cats are living beings; each is an individual with his own personality. You can't buy one "off the shelf," pre-programmed to be the perfect pet you envision. You can choose your preferred color and type, but to a great extent, the way the cat behaves and relates to you will depend on the way you care for, handle, and interact with him. Some pedigreed cats are known for certain character traits, such as a laid-back attitude and a strong affection for humans, and this can make the job of choosing a cat easier.

Types of cats

All domestic cats, whatever their color, coat length, or temperament, fall into one of three main groups.

1 Pedigreed (purebred)

These cats are bred from pedigreed parents of the same breed. The advantage of getting a purebred cat is that you know what he will look like when he is fully grown and, providing you have checked out information about the breed, you'll have a good idea of his typical temperament and characteristics as an adult.

2 Cross-bred

Such cats are the offspring of pedigreed parents, but of different breeds—for example, a Persian crossed with a British Shorthair. The resulting kittens could grow up to resemble either parent or be a mixture of both. Some could be longhaired, some shorthaired, and some semi-longhaired.

3 Non-pedigreed

Cats are described as non-pedigreed if one or both parents were cross-breeds. Different breeds may have been mixed over generations, which can make the appearance, personality, and temperament of offspring difficult to predict.

Top tip

Pedigreed cats are not necessarily any more loving, clever, or naughty than other cats, and their beauty is a matter of taste. Orientals tend to be more demanding of their owners, Persians seem to be more laid-back, and non-pedigreeds are generally thought of as being "hardy." Whatever the type or breeding, an animal's personality is also determined by the way he is reared and his handling by humans. Whether you get a pedigreed or non-pedigreed cat, the costs of neutering, vaccinating, feeding, and caring for him will be just the same. The only difference will be the initial cost of acquiring him.

AT-A-GLANCE PEDIGREED CATS

TYPE	PROS	CONS
Pedigreed 	• Having researched the breed, you can pinpoint your ideal pet, usually knowing what to expect in terms of appearance and personality. • Many types and colors exist, appealing to individual tastes. • You can choose the type and color you want, although you may have to wait a while for your exact requirement. • Pedigreed cats are usually raised with the greatest of care, so you should expect a healthy animal.	• Pedigreed cats are more expensive than cross-breeds. • Some breeds are prone to hereditary problems or particular ailments (especially those bred to "type"). • Some breeds have particular personality traits or care requirements that may not be appealing to you or practical for your lifestyle. • Certain breeds can be difficult to obtain if they are rare or the demand exceeds availability.
Cross-bred 	• Usually less expensive than purebreds. • If you know what the parents are like, you'll have a fair idea of what to expect in terms of appearance and personality. • Generally more hardy than purebreds, but this does depend on the cross and the genetic parentage. • Because the crosses are usually intended, you can normally expect the resulting animals to be well socialized and healthy. Do be aware, though, that this is not always the case.	• They are not always readily available, especially if you want a very specific cross-breed. • Due to the personality and behavior traits of the breeds involved, certain combinations can be quite explosive, such as Burmese crossed with Siamese. Both breeds are attention-seeking types, highly active and vocal, so the combination can result in an extremely demanding pet! Some owners may enjoy this, while others could find such an animal exhausting and infuriating.
Non-pedigreed	• Free or inexpensive. • Wide type and color choice. • Usually widely available. • Generally uncomplicated in terms of health.	• The traits of the parents are generally unknown, so how the cat will mature in terms of looks, behavior, and personality is hard to predict. • You may have to look for a while to find the age, color, and sex of your choice. • You can't always be sure that the animal has been properly raised and cared for, so look for signs of ill health and behavior problems.

Coat lengths

There are two types of coat: shorthaired and longhaired (the latter is often incorrectly referred to as Persian, which is a breed in its own right). Each is exactly as the name suggests, although some coats are thicker than others, depending on the breed of cat. There are also "hairless" cats (such as the Sphynx), which have only a thin covering of down on the ears, muzzle, tail, and—in the males—testicles. Semi-longhaired coats are not as thick, nor as long in some cases, as longhaired coats. Some breeds have curly coats (Cornish Rex, Selkirk Rex, and La Perm, which can be either long- or shorthaired).

Coat colors

Cat coats come in many different colors, with purebreds boasting the most variations. The basic colors of the cat are simple to interpret—black, white, cream, and silver, for instance—but others are more obscure (see the chart below).

Cream

COATS OF MANY COLORS

Bi-color A white coat with dark patches.

Blue Any shade of cold-toned gray.

Blue-cream Dilute version of tortie with a mingled or patched coat of palest gray and cream. There are other color varieties, including chocolate-cream, lilac-cream, and so on.

Bronze Warm, coppery brown that lightens to buff.

Blue

Brown Any shade of dark brown, except in a brown tabby, when it refers to a cat who is genetically black and has black markings on an agouti (grizzled, like a wild rabbit) background.

Cameo White fur with red tips.

Caramel A subtle shade of pale orangey brown.

Champagne Buff-cream with warm honey beige shading to pale gold tan.

Chinchilla White coat with tips of a darker color.

Red colorpoint

Chocolate A rich, warm brown.

Cinnamon Lighter shades of chocolate.

Colorpoint Solid body with tail, paws, mask (face), and ears of another color.

Harlequin A bi-color coat: 50–75 percent white; 25–50 percent color.

Lilac Very pale, warm-toned gray.

Mink A range of colors in the Tonkinese breed.

Solid

Frequently asked question

Q Which coat type is preferable—shorthaired, longhaired, or semi-longhaired?

A You may prefer the look of a semi-longhaired or longhaired cat, but will you have the time and inclination to keep his coat looking good and tangle-free on a daily basis? Can you cope with the amount of hair a long-coated cat may shed around the house? Longhaired cats need grooming every single day to keep their coats and skin in top order, whereas shorthaired cats take care of most of the necessary daily grooming themselves. Although the latter shed hair, too, they do so less profusely than their long-coated counterparts.

Parti-color Covers both bi-colors and torties.

Patched Two-tone tabby coat with darker and lighter patches, mingling tortie and tabby. Patched is sometimes also referred to as tortie, which can be confusing.

Platinum Pale, silvery gray with pale fawn undertones.

Red All shades of ginger. Deep coppery tones are the most sought after.

Ruddy A modification of black in the Abyssinian breed to reddish brown and burnt sienna.

Sable A term sometimes used to describe dark brown cats who are genetically black.

Smoke White undercoat, with topcoat hair white at the roots and colored at the ends.

Solid One color.

Sorrel Modification of red in the Abyssinian to brownish orange and light brown.

Tabby There are four basic patterns: *ticked* (each hair has contrasting dark and light color bands), *mackerel* (vertically striped; also called tiger), *spotted* (as it suggests), and *classic* (sides are blotched with whorls or "oyster" marks).

Tipped Hairs are differently colored only at the ends, which can create a sparkling effect.

Tortie-and-White (Calico) Tri-colored (black, red, and white).

Tortie (Tortoiseshell) A two-colored (black and red) coat.

Tuxedo Black with white paws, chest, and belly.

Classic silver tabby

Blue, tortie, and white

Appearance

Cats come in all shapes and sizes to suit all requirements and tastes. Examples include the Munchkin, with its short legs (said to be excellent house pets because they're unable to jump onto kitchen counters); the Scottish Fold, which has folded ears; the American Curl, with curled ears; the Manx, which has no tail; the Japanese Bobtail, which sports a short, curly tail (called a pom); and the lynx-like American Bobtail, with its unusual voice.

Your lifestyle

This determines, to a great extent, what sort of pet you should be looking for. In the cat's lifetime, you are responsible for his health and mental well-being. Obviously, if you're going to be away from home for more than a day or so, you need to find someone to check on the cat and provide fresh food, water, and litter.

Some breeds are very high-maintenance compared to others, so consider these types only if you are able to provide properly for them for the next 15 years or so. If you acquire a longhaired cat, you must be prepared to learn how to care for his coat properly; if you choose an extroverted, energetic type, you must have the time to give him all the attention he needs. Such considerations may seem obvious, but animal welfare organizations still have to cope with

A Sphynx's skin should look like velvet and feel like moss. Because he has no protective coat, he must be kept in comfortably warm conditions. He also has no eyebrows or whiskers.

If you want a pedigreed cat to show, be sure to choose an excellent example of the breed, but expect to pay a premium price for him.

This "Peke-faced" Persian may be desirable on the show bench, but "typey" cats (those with grossly exaggerated features) are often prone to respiratory and other problems due to their physical abnormalities. In addition, some breeds (or breeding lines) display certain characteristic behavior traits that may not be desirable to some people, so it pays to thoroughly research the breed you're interested in. If possible, speak to other owners, vets, and breeders before making a final decision.

thousands of pet cats who are abandoned because their owners felt unable to care for them properly.

Ultimately, picking a pedigreed or non-pedigreed cat is your decision. You are in the best position to make an informed choice so you end up with a pet who is the right color and type. How you will turn your chosen cat into the ideal companion you desire, given your lifestyle and expectations of him, is detailed in the following pages.

Feline fact

The trend for establishing different breeds of cat began early in the twentieth century, and there are now more than 50 distinctive pedigreed breeds and hundreds of color varieties.

Longhaired cats need regular grooming to keep their coats tangle-free and their skin in good condition. Long coats can hide a multitude of problems, such as ticks and weight loss or gain, so it's essential to check for these regularly.

Kitten or adult?

Many people automatically think of acquiring a kitten, but that may not be the best choice for their circumstances or lifestyle; it's easier to see the character of an older cat, and any difficult or undesirable traits will already be apparent. Consider the points on the checklist before making a decision.

Checklist
- ✓ your lifestyle
- ✓ your circumstances
- ✓ your available time
- ✓ your requirements
- ✓ your other pets (if applicable)
- ✓ age considerations (human and animal)

AT-A-GLANCE CAT-AGE CHECKLIST

AGE	PROS	CONS
Kitten	• Kittens and young adults tend to be more adaptable than their mature counterparts, but it really does depend on circumstances and their personalities. • You can enjoy seeing him grow and develop. • You will, with luck, have many years to enjoy together. • You can train him to behave in the way you want. • If you get two kittens, they will provide company for each other.	• You need to give a young kitten several meals at regular intervals through the day, as well as more attention, so he may prove very time-consuming. • Being introduced into a busy family may be frightening, unless he's been brought up in such an environment and been well socialized with humans (and possibly other pets) since birth. • If there are young children in the house, a kitten is less able to defend himself or escape from them if need be. • He has not been neutered.
Adult	• An adult cat is not as time-consuming as a kitten. • His personality is already established. • He is probably socialized with other humans and animals. • He is probably neutered.	• He may take longer to bond with you and your family and/or other pets. • He may have a limited life span, depending on his age. • He may be more difficult to integrate into your family. • He may have a disease or other ailment. • He may have undesirable behavior traits.

Frequently asked question

Q Which would be better—a male or a female?

A If your cat or kitten is to be neutered, the question of sex becomes much less important. Neutered males may be larger than females, but there is little difference otherwise. Males, especially those who are neutered, are said to be more loving toward their owners, but much depends on the way the cat is brought up and treated by his owner, as females can be just as affectionate. For more information on neutering, see pages 140–43.

Cats and children

Children age three and under can't be expected to know how to approach and handle a cat correctly, so close supervision is the best way of preventing them from being scratched. Naturally, children of all ages want to explore their new pet and establish a relationship with him, but poking him in the ear or disturbing him while he is asleep are not good ways to do that. If young people are taught how to handle cats with gentleness and respect, most children and cats become the best of friends. See pages 94–95 for more information on this subject.

One cat or more?

Your cat will be much happier with a companion, whether it is another cat or other pet, especially if you're away from home for many hours. However, this is usually only the case if they have been brought up together. If you're thinking about having two

For the safety of both parties, never allow a child to grab at or chase your cat or kitten.

cats, it would be better to get a couple of similarly aged kittens, or two adults who are used to living with each other, at the outset. See pages 82–83 for detailed information about introducing a second cat.

Sexing cats

Female (near right): *The vulva is the vertical opening immediately below the anus; it looks as though it is almost joined to the anus.*

Male (far right): *As in the female, the anus is immediately below the tail; the scrotal sac containing the testicles is below this, with the penis concealed in the opening below the scrotal sac.*

When to get a cat

Thinking about getting a cat and actually getting one can be two very different things. Whether you opt for an adult cat or a kitten, you must take into account your personal circumstances at the time. You may want a cat desperately, but would a cat want to be with you at this moment in your life? See the checklist for things to consider.

Checklist

✓ availability of kittens or cats
✓ vacation plans
✓ work commitments
✓ stress levels
✓ pregnancy
✓ time of year
✓ family commitments
✓ financial situation

Timing

The time is not ideal to get a cat if you are:
• moving
• hectically busy at work and socially
• changing jobs or losing a job
• dealing with an illness
• separating from your partner
• mourning a death in the family
• expecting a new baby
• due to go on vacation
• about to celebrate something that will result in upheaval of the family routine

Of course, there are always exceptions to the rules, and many people find comfort in their pets at times of great stress. Such owners may feel that, although they are in turmoil, their pets are not suffering in any way because they remain fed and cared for. However, animals do feel their owners' anxieties (this is called anxiety transference) and feel worried themselves. This may manifest in unusual behavior such as attention seeking or soiling around the house, or the cat may even disappear for a while (some even abandon the family home completely). It's important, therefore, to ensure that you are in a position both materially and emotionally to offer a secure and harmonious home to a cat.

Frequently asked question

Q I want to get a cat, but I am expecting a baby. Is it best to get a cat before or after the birth?

A It's probably better to wait until you have had the baby before introducing a new pet. This way, the new cat will view the infant as one of the family rather than an unwelcome intrusion into his life. If you have a cat, toxoplasmosis (see page 97) can be a concern to new mothers, but, providing you worm your pet correctly and adhere to household hygiene rules, this risk should be minimal.

Vacations

Wait until you have been on vacation before getting a cat, because otherwise he will suffer upheaval twice in a very short time—initially when you remove him from his former home, and then when you disappear for a while and either leave him in a kennel or with a trusted caretaker. To remain mentally and physically well, a new pet needs a good deal of time to settle in and feel secure in his new home before anything out of the ordinary occurs, such as being displaced, even for a short while.

Availability

Sometimes it's not as easy to get a cat as you may imagine, for several reasons:
• If you desire a particular breed, color, or sex of cat or kitten, it may not be available "on spec"; you may have to

Did you know...?

• Insecure cats who feel anxious or threatened in their home, for whatever reason, may spray urine or deposit feces around the property. Doing this fills their "territories" with their own individual scents and helps them feel safer.
• It takes time to get to know new owners and territory well, which is why cats can be so unsettled for the first six months in a new home.

reserve your specific requirement with a breeder (or even several breeders) so that when such cats become available, you have first choice.
• Availability of kittens is dependent on breeding seasons.
• Kittens tend to be in high demand at animal shelters, so you may have to wait until one becomes available.
• You may not find the exact type of cat you want at shelters right away, so be prepared to wait.

Whether young or old, cats are adorable, and it would be very easy to get one on impulse, but it's important to restrain yourself and consider whether the time is right to get a feline friend.

Top tip

Before you get a cat, consider the benefits you can offer him rather than the benefits you think he can offer you.

Where to get a cat

There are many places to investigate when searching for a feline friend, such as breeders of pedigreed cats, owners of a non-pedigreed cat who has had kittens, and animal shelters. Which one you choose to explore is your decision, but it helps to be fully informed of the potential advantages and disadvantages of each before you do so.

Checklist
- ✓ breeders
- ✓ newspaper ads
- ✓ animal shelters
- ✓ adopting a stray
- ✓ pet stores
- ✓ friends and family

Finding a cat

Your local paper, pet stores, bulletin boards at vets' offices, cat magazines, word-of-mouth through friends and family, and shelters are all potential sources for finding a cat or kitten. If you want a kitten, bear in mind that he needs to be at least eight weeks old before he can safely leave his mother. By this time, he should be fully weaned onto kitten food and ideally be socialized with a wide range of people and other animals. Some breeders prefer to wait until their kittens are 12 weeks old so that they are fully litter-trained and have had their initial vaccinations.

Top tip

Some cats are naturally quiet and staid in their habits, while others are extroverted clowns. It's possible that you will see both types in the same litter. A noisy, busy household with young children and other pets is not the place for a timid and sensitive cat or kitten, while an outgoing, mischievous feline may prove a little too lively for a quiet home.

If you know of a friend or neighbor whose cat has recently given birth, this may be a good place to start if you're thinking about acquiring a cat. You will already be familiar with the mother cat and know whether she is healthy and has a good temperament.

Cat shows are held on a regular basis in many countries and can be one- or two-day events. Entry to shows as a spectator is not expensive, and breeders who are exhibiting are usually listed in the show catalog.

Which source is best?

No one source is best, as there are considerations to take into account with all of them.

Breeders

When obtaining a kitten (pedigreed or not) from a breeder, try to select him from a whole litter, if possible. The appearance of the young cats will influence your choice, but so too should their behavior and health. It's preferable to pick one who appears healthy (see page 28); is outgoing, frisky, and friendly; and approaches you confidently. Avoid taking an animal who looks unhealthy (see page 29) since you may be taking on a problem; take your time and look elsewhere for a cat instead.

HOW MUCH WILL HE COST?

SOURCE	COSTS
Animal shelter	• There is generally a charge to cover the cost of neutering and vaccinations.
Breeder	• Depending on the breed and whether the cat is of show quality, prices can vary enormously.
Friends or family	• Non-pedigreed kittens or adult cats are generally "free to good homes"; purebreds and part-purebreds can vary, depending on the reason the owners are offering them.
Pet store	• Prices vary: pedigreed cats are more expensive than non-pedigreed.
Stray	• Free.

If you find what you think is a stray, make inquiries before taking him in to ensure he is actually homeless and not someone's much-loved pet. Many cats wander away from their homes as they explore their territory, and sociable ones will happily come into your home for a tasty free meal and some affection even though they are well fed and cared for at home. Old cats tend to look a bit disheveled, and their coats may not always be in good condition, so it's quite possible to mistake such an animal for a stray.

Sometimes it's possible to get an older pedigreed pet from a breeder who has no further need for a particular cat, or kittens resulting from accidental matings and not suited to a breeding program. Breeders sometimes insist that such cats be neutered so they can't breed.

Friends or family

Opting for an older cat can be a good idea if you don't have much time to spend training a kitten, particularly if you are offered a well-behaved animal by a family member or friend.

Frequently asked question

Q We would like to get a pedigreed cat, but we're unsure about which breed would be best. Without traveling far and wide to see different breeders, how can we learn what the different breeds are and what they look like?

A It's a good idea to visit a championship cat show, where you will see many different ages, breeds, and colors all under one roof. You can see how a particular breed of kitten will mature, and you may be able to glean information about the types you are particularly drawn to. You will find shows advertised in cat magazines. If traveling to a show isn't possible, get a good book on cat breeds. Once you decide on a breed, check cat magazines or the Internet for contact information for breed organizations and individual breeders.

Did you know...?

Kittens are not always available all year round; fewer are born in late winter than during the spring and summer months.

Although your time together may be limited, an older cat has much to offer in terms of affection and companionship. Don't discount an "oldster," as there are many in shelters seeking loving homes in which to live out their days.

Animal shelter

If you decide to choose a pet from an animal shelter, find out as much as you can from the staff about his background. Some cats, for example, may not be litter-trained if they have spent their lives roaming about on their own, and such animals may not integrate well into a domestic environment. If a cat's age is unknown, there are no reliable indicators for determining how old he is.

Stray cats

Sometimes a cat simply moves into a home where he finds a welcome, or you may come across one you think has been abandoned. However, if you do find a "stray," be aware that someone somewhere could be grieving over the disappearance of their pet. Make every effort to trace his owners by informing the local authorities and animal shelters, by putting up "found" posters in local stores and veterinary clinics, and by having the animal checked for a microchip at the vet's. Once you have satisfied yourself that he is indeed a stray, have him checked over by a vet to ensure he is healthy, and have him neutered if necessary.

Pet stores

Buying a cat from a pet store can be risky, so be especially critical. Be sure that the animals in the store look well cared for; have adequate space, food, and water; and appear healthy. If many cats are kept together in a less-than-ideal environment, and there is a constant turnover of "stock," there's a high risk of infection being present, and you may find yourself with a sick pet.

Feline fact

If you pick a cat from an animal shelter, you'll have the satisfaction of finding a pet as well as the knowledge that you've probably saved a life, since many unwanted pets must be destroyed. Elderly cats are more difficult to adopt out than their younger counterparts, so if you require a quiet, laid-back pet, do consider a mature cat.

Signs of a healthy cat

Alert, calm demeanor • Supple movement • Normal body weight

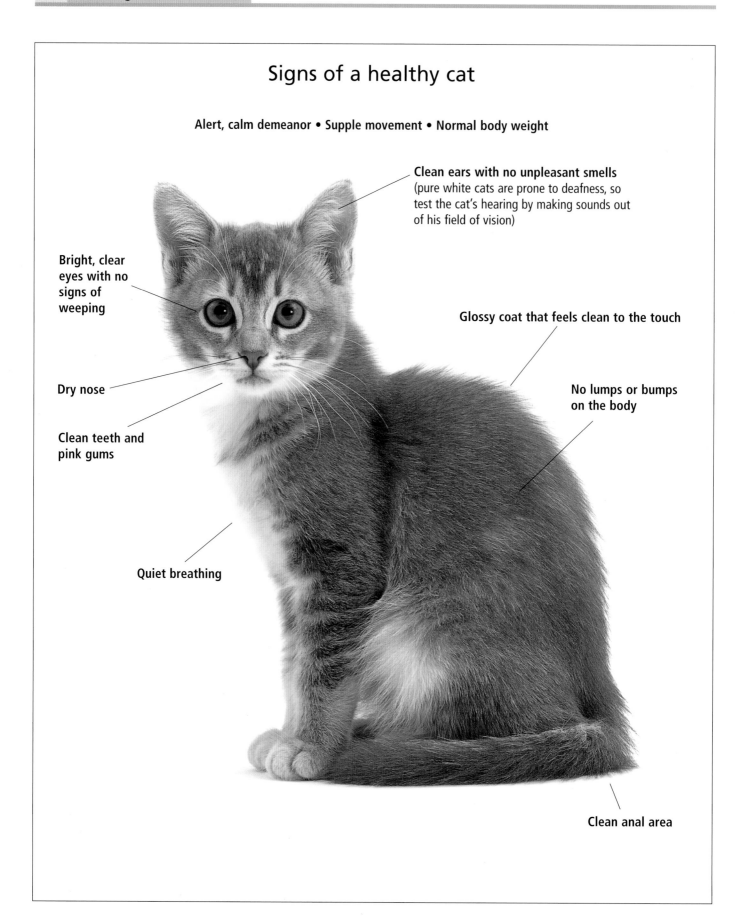

Clean ears with no unpleasant smells
(pure white cats are prone to deafness, so
test the cat's hearing by making sounds out
of his field of vision)

**Bright, clear
eyes with no
signs of
weeping**

Glossy coat that feels clean to the touch

Dry nose

**No lumps or bumps
on the body**

**Clean teeth and
pink gums**

Quiet breathing

Clean anal area

Signs of an unhealthy cat

Depressed demeanor • Constant scratching • Abnormal body weight

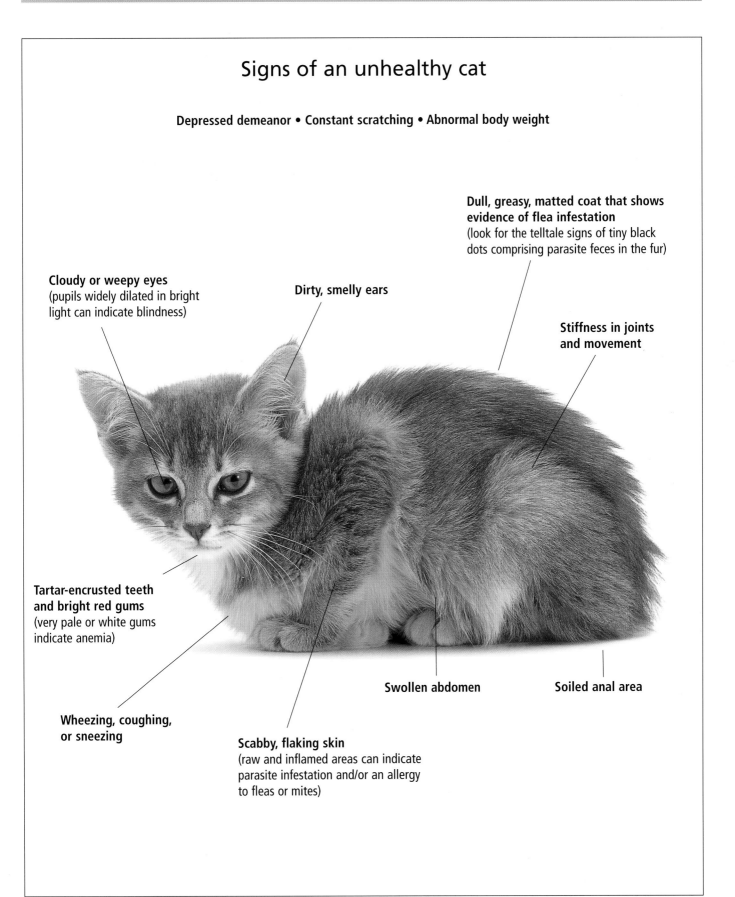

Dull, greasy, matted coat that shows evidence of flea infestation
(look for the telltale signs of tiny black dots comprising parasite feces in the fur)

Cloudy or weepy eyes
(pupils widely dilated in bright light can indicate blindness)

Dirty, smelly ears

Stiffness in joints and movement

Tartar-encrusted teeth and bright red gums
(very pale or white gums indicate anemia)

Swollen abdomen

Soiled anal area

Wheezing, coughing, or sneezing

Scabby, flaking skin
(raw and inflamed areas can indicate parasite infestation and/or an allergy to fleas or mites)

Essential equipment

The vast array of equipment and products designed for cats—many marketed as being something your pet just can't live without—can be bewildering for a new or prospective owner. However, many of these items are simply not essential. As long as your cat is warm; has somewhere to rest comfortably, safely, and undisturbed; is fed regularly; has a constant supply of fresh, clean water; has somewhere suitable to relieve himself; and has some toys to play with, he will be perfectly happy.

You don't need a great deal of equipment to care for your new cat or kitten, and what you do need tends to be inexpensive. The checklist shows the basic things you will need, although you can add items as you require them.

Checklist

- ✓ food and water bowls
- ✓ litter box and litter
- ✓ bed and bedding
- ✓ toys
- ✓ first-aid kit (see pages 157–58)
- ✓ collar and ID tag
- ✓ carrier
- ✓ scratching post

Food and water bowls

Your cat should have his own food and water bowls (see page 42), placed on a plastic "placemat" or piece of newspaper to catch any spills. You can buy automatic feeding bowls that dispense dry food at pre-set times. Pedal bowls, if your cat learns how to use them, can also be handy; these are lidded bowls that open when your cat puts a paw on the pedal mechanism and close when he takes it off.

Litter box and litter

A litter box is essential even if you allow your cat to go outside. There are two basic types—open and covered (hooded). Covered types prevent the litter from being scattered outside the box, contain smells better, and afford the cat more privacy. However, some cats don't like to be enclosed and will use only an open box.

Choose a box big enough for your cat and one that will hold a good depth of litter; cats like to bury their wastes completely, without wetting or soiling their paws. Lining the box with newspaper or a plastic liner will make cleaning it out much easier. Place the box on newspaper or a piece of vinyl floor covering so that any spills will be easy to clean up.

Litter types include (clockwise from top) clay-based litter, fine-grain litter with a grit/sand-like consistency, and wood-based litter made from sawdust or paper pellets.

AT-A-GLANCE CAT LITTER

LITTER TYPE*	PROS	CONS
Clay or sand-based	• Inexpensive • Absorbs moisture efficiently	• Doesn't absorb smells • Cheaper varieties can leave heavy tracking when wet • Heavy to carry
Newspaper	• Inexpensive • Readily available	• Not very absorbent • Ink can stain a cat's feet and, therefore, carpet and furniture • Ink ingested when cat washes can cause illness • Any newspaper lying around the house may be considered a bathroom area
Paper or wood pellets	• Efficiently absorb moisture and smells • Non-staining • Light to carry	• Expensive
Scented (clay or scoopable)	• Helps to mask smells	• More expensive than unscented • Can be too strong-smelling, which is off-putting to cat and owner • Scenting may make it tempting not to wash the box as often • Scented chemicals can irritate the cat's respiratory system and foot pads
Scoopable	• Lasts longer, since all wastes can be scooped and discarded • Minimizes smells	• Initially expensive • Heavy to carry
Silica crystals	• Soak up urine like a sponge • Virtually eliminate litter-box smells • Easy to maintain: Simply remove solid waste daily and change the whole box of crystals every few weeks • Non-staining • Light to carry	• Initially expensive • Can be tricky to clean up if it gets on the floor
Wheat husk	• Absorbs well • Lasts longer, since it clumps and wastes can be discarded	• Initially expensive

*Some types may not be available in certain areas

Dispose of used litter, well wrapped in newspaper or biodegradable bags, with your household trash, not down the toilet, since this could cause a blockage. Consult your vet or local waste-disposal company about disposing of waste from a cat who is receiving radiation treatment.

Bed and bedding

There are many types of cat beds (see chart on opposite page). Blankets, fleece material, a cushion or old pillow, and fleecy veterinary pet bedding are all good, insulating materials. Wash bedding regularly to remove dirt and help prevent flea infestation.

A warm, cozy bed in which to curl up will be much appreciated by your cat.

AT-A-GLANCE CAT BEDS

BED TYPE*	PROS	CONS
Beanbag	• Comfortable • Warm • Cats love them	• Can be time-consuming to remove the polystyrene beads in order to wash the cover • If the beads escape, they're not easy to clean up
Cardboard box	• Cheap • Readily available • High sides keep out drafts	• Need replacing regularly • Need bedding
Covered (hooded)	• Most cats feel secure in them • Draft-free • No bedding needed with cushioned types	• Can be difficult to wash and dry • Expensive • Some cats don't like being enclosed
Cushioned or fake-fur	• Comfortable • No bedding usually needed	• Can harbor fleas if not washed regularly • Can be difficult to wash and dry • Expensive
Over-the-radiator cradle	• Space-saving • Great for cats who need extra warmth (very young, old, ill, hairless) • Being raised off the floor gives sense of security	• Stiff-jointed cats may not be able to access them easily • May harbor fleas if not washed regularly
Plastic	• Inexpensive • Hygienic • Easy to clean • High-sided types keep out drafts	• Need bedding
Wicker	• Looks attractive ***Some types may not be available in certain areas.**	• Expensive • Drafty • Harbor dust and fur; difficult to clean • Cats tend to scratch them to bits • Need bedding

A hooded bed can provide a sense of privacy and security, particularly in a busy household.

Toys

Playing with your cat is rewarding for both of you. Cats play most during kittenhood, and if they learn to play with toys during this time, they will probably continue to do so during adulthood. Moving toys in ways that mimic prey behavior will result in more fun for your cat and more interest for you. Darting movements from side to side in front of the cat, rather than up-and-down movements, are more likely to result in play. Toys that move erratically or very fast,

There is a huge variety of toys on the market that are specially designed for cats and mimic the behavior of prey when rolled, rustled, dangled, and dragged along the ground.

Some cats, Siamese in particular, can be trained to walk on a leash. For this, you will need a harness and a leash designed for cats. Various versions are available, from plain to intricately decorated, and in different colors, but the first considerations are that the harness is comfortable for your cat and the leash is long enough for comfort and ease of movement for both parties.

then are stationary, are more likely to be "hunted." Many stuffed toys contain the herb catnip (also called catmint), which cats find irresistible.

Collar and ID tag

Ideally, if your cat goes outdoors, he should wear a reflective or fluorescent collar complete with an ID tag and a bell to warn wildlife and birds of his presence. Collars are available in many styles and colors, but you should always use one with either an elastic insert or a quick-release fastening (which opens under pressure) for safety in case your cat becomes caught on something.

When fitting a collar, make sure you can slide two fingers between it and the cat's neck. Check the collar regularly for signs of chafing and to be sure that it still fits comfortably on a growing cat.

Carrier

For trips to the vet or anywhere else, you'll need a cat carrier. There are several types, but whatever you choose should be easy to handle and carry with your cat inside, and it must close securely so he can't escape.

Cardboard carriers are cheap and are fine for occasional use, but they won't hold a cat who's determined to get out, and they're liable to break if wet. Wicker carriers, while attractive, are hard to clean and not as long-wearing as other types.

Rigid carriers made of high-impact plastic and wire-mesh "kennels" are sturdy and secure and come in several sizes. Both front- and top-opening plastic types are available; they're draft-free, reasonably light, and easy to clean. Wire-mesh crates are ideal for cats who dislike being enclosed, and since most open from the top,

Scratching post

Every cat has a biological need to scratch in order to help keep his claws in good working order. Unless you provide your cat with something he can scratch to his heart's content, such as a scratching post, he will inevitably exercise his claws on your furniture. Help train your cat to use the post by rubbing it with catnip (crush a little fresh catnip in your hands and rub them on the post) or by spraying it with catnip essence (available from pet stores).

Make sure your cat's scratching post is stable when in use.

Plastic-coated wire-mesh carriers are available in several sizes. Large ones are useful if you have two or more cats to transport.

Top tip

If your cat has a preference for a chair or sofa arm on which to scratch, then, when you replace the item, keep that arm as a homemade scratching post that your cat will be familiar with. This may keep him from transferring the habit to your new furniture.

Indoor crate

Although not absolutely essential, an indoor crate can prove extremely useful. A crate designed for dogs can afford more space if necessary. The crate provides a secure den during a cat's integration period in a new home and makes his introduction to existing pets more manageable and less traumatic. When you can't be around to supervise young kittens, popping them into the crate will keep them safely away from wires and other hazards.

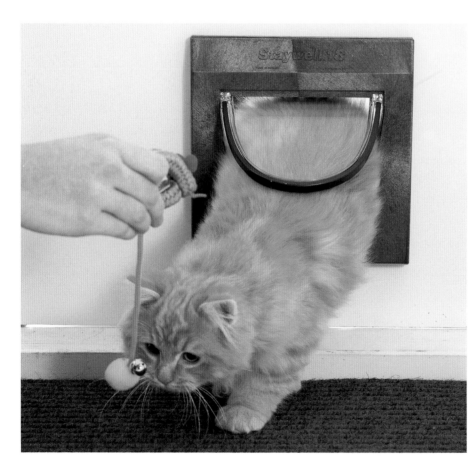

A crate or pen should be large enough for the cat to move around freely and should accommodate toys, a litter box, and food and water bowls. If you want one for only a short period, it may be possible to rent one from a vet or breeder.

Some types of cat flaps can be set into walls; this is handy if you don't want to put one in a door or window.

they make loading and unloading easier. (This type may not be available in some areas.)

Nylon carriers resemble airline carry-on bags, with mesh panels for ventilation and visibility. Most open from the top, usually with zippers, and are foldable and easy to store. These bags are lighter than rigid types, but the flexibility of some models makes it more difficult to load a cat who's reluctant to be confined.

Cat flap

A cat flap fitted into an outside door or window will, when unlocked, allow your pet to enter and leave the house at leisure. Various designs are available, including electromagnetic and electronically operated flaps that will open only to a cat with a special device attached to his collar. Fit the cat flap low enough in the door or window for your pet to be able to use it comfortably, and install it far enough away from the handle or lock to prevent burglars from reaching inside and letting themselves in.

Parasite treatments

You will need to treat your cat for internal and external parasites on a regular basis. The best treatments are available only from vets, but they're worth spending a little bit more on because they work efficiently, unlike many store-bought products. See page 138 for more detailed information.

Top tip

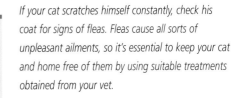

Don't use a flea collar at the same time as other flea treatments, or you may overexpose your pet to the chemicals they contain, which can make him ill.

If your cat scratches himself constantly, check his coat for signs of fleas. Fleas cause all sorts of unpleasant ailments, so it's essential to keep your cat and home free of them by using suitable treatments obtained from your vet.

Feeding

Feeding your cat a well-balanced diet and the right amount of food on a daily basis is essential for his good health. These days, the pet-food industry is big business, and there is a wide range of feline foods available—many of which are aggressively marketed—so it can be difficult deciding which variety or brand is the best choice for your pet. There are, however, certain dietary nutrients that a cat can't do without, and these are shown on the checklist. Taking these and your cat's age, health, and lifestyle into account when purchasing cat food can help make it easier to decide which diet is most suitable.

Checklist

- ✓ vitamin A
- ✓ B vitamins (especially niacin)
- ✓ vitamin D
- ✓ vitamin E
- ✓ calcium
- ✓ phosphorus
- ✓ protein
- ✓ iodine
- ✓ amino acids (especially taurine)
- ✓ fats
- ✓ fiber
- ✓ water
- ✓ grass

A need for meat

Cats are known as "obligate carnivores," meaning that they depend on meat and similar foods, such as fish, as sources of vital nutrients in order to remain healthy. Unable to exist on a low-protein diet, cats need relatively large amounts of meat-based food per day in relation to their size. In the wild, a cat hunts, kills, feeds, and then rests. He may gorge himself on a whole rabbit or several mice and birds on one day, then go without food completely for the next two or three days. Adult domestic cats are usually fed once a day, but splitting that feeding into two meals adds interaction and interest and alleviates boredom. Don't feed your cat dog food, as this is formulated for canine nutritional needs, not feline ones.

Necessary nutrients

It's important to ensure that the balance of nutrients fed to a cat is correct, since excesses can cause as many health problems as deficiencies can. This is why it is better to feed quality commercially prepared foods rather than a home-made diet through which it's difficult to be sure your cat is receiving all the correct nutrients. For example, a diet of cooked carcass meat alone is low in calcium, vitamin A, and iodine, and these deficiencies may lead to osteoporosis (brittle bone disease). A liver-rich diet can cause excess vitamin A, resulting in bony outgrowths around the joints and spine that make movement painful.

Carbohydrates

Although they can digest and metabolize cooked carbohydrates, cats have no nutritional need for them because their necessarily high-protein diet supplies all the energy they require. However, foods such as breakfast cereals can provide a useful source of energy.

Vitamins

A relatively high level of vitamin A is needed to keep body cells working properly. Vitamins of the B group are important for the maintenance of the central nervous system. Vitamin D helps the body produce calcium, which is essential for healthy bones and teeth, although cats need far

Eating grass

Cats eat grass as a source of folate, a B vitamin. Grass also acts as an emetic to induce vomiting and rid the stomach of hairballs, worms, and other causes of digestive upset.

Top tips

How much to feed
Follow the manufacturer's instructions on the food packaging; they're generally a good guide to what amount of food to feed per day at each life stage. You can split this amount into as many meals as you wish throughout the day, depending on your pet's preference and your daily routine.

Supplements
On a commercially prepared and therefore carefully formulated and balanced diet, your cat shouldn't need any food supplements (vitamins, minerals, and oils), unless your vet advises you to use them. Overdosing on nutrients can be detrimental to your pet's health.

less than dogs or humans. Phosphorus is also essential for healthy bones and teeth, while vitamin E helps prevent cell damage. Since cats can produce vitamin C (ascorbic acid; essential for maintaining healthy connective tissue and skin) in their bodies, it does not need to be included in the diet.

Proteins

Proteins present in meat help build body tissue, carry out "repairs," and make hormones. They also supply essential amino acids that a cat's own body can't produce, one of which is taurine. A deficiency of taurine results in visual impairment, infertility, and heart disease.

Fats

Dietary fats comprise a concentrated energy source of all nutrients and supply the essential fatty acids (EFAs) that are vital in maintaining total-body health.

Fiber

A lack of fiber in the diet, especially in elderly, inactive cats, can cause constipation and other digestive problems caused by sluggish bowels. Quality commercial foods supply adequate fiber; other sources include cooked vegetables and cereal foods.

Commercially produced adult and kitten foods are available in (top to bottom) wet/moist, semi-moist, and dry forms. Try each type to find out which one your cat prefers.

Food types

Good-quality commercial foods are the easiest to feed. They contain all the necessary nutrients in the correct proportions, including vitamins and minerals, which could be lacking in a homemade diet of fresh or cooked meat and table scraps. There are three forms of commercially prepared food.

1 Wet/moist (canned or pouch)

Canned food has a high water content, is available in a wide range of flavors, and is often preferred by cats.

2 Semi-moist (pouch)

Often containing vegetable protein, such as soy, this food type contains less water than canned and therefore keeps well in a bowl without drying out and losing texture.

3 Dry (box or bag)

As its name suggests, dry food contains minimal water, so your cat will need plenty of water to drink in conjunction with it. Because of its hard, crunchy texture, dry food helps keep cats' teeth tartar-free and in good condition. However, it's best to use it as only part of the diet because some cats become addicted to it, and it can contribute to urinary problems.

Frequently asked question

Q I have heard that dry foods can cause crystal formation in the urine, leading to urinary tract problems. Is this true?

A Dry foods got some bad press when they first came on the market, as they were linked to feline urological syndrome (FUS), also known as feline lower urinary tract disease (FLUTD). It was more common in inactive cats who ate only a dry diet and drank little water. The condition meant that the cat strained to pass urine but was unable to because crystals in the urine partially or totally blocked the tube from the bladder. The formula for dry cat foods was changed, and they are now widely used, although it's preferable to choose high-quality brands to ensure the formula balance is correct and to interchange dry food with moist food regularly. Fresh water should always be available. (Some vets also advise against regularly feeding seafood, since it may contribute to FLUTD.)

Life-stage feeding

Different feeding regimens are appropriate for the various stages in a cat's life (see chart below).

If you feed your cat outside, always do so in a secure place where no other animal can share or steal his dinner.

Life-cycle feeding

From birth to weaning	Kittens usually stop drinking their mother's milk and go on to solid food when they are 8 weeks old; gradual weaning starts at 4–5 weeks. After that, they should be fed kitten food, as this contains all the essential nutrients they need in a form that's easy for them to digest and utilize. Fed correctly at this age, they are on course to grow into healthy, well-developed adults.
From weaning to 12 weeks	Five small meals a day, each of around 1 oz (28 g).
From 12 to 20 weeks	Four meals a day.
From 20 to 30 weeks	Three meals a day.
From 30 weeks to 12 months (juvenile/adolescent)	Gradually reduce to two meals a day.
From 12 months to 8 years (adult)	One or two meals a day.
From 8 years onward (elderly)	One or two meals a day, but you may have to increase to two or more depending on your pet's overall condition.

QUICK-REFERENCE FEEDING GUIDE

Age of cat	Body weight	Daily food requirements	Feedings per day
Newborn	4 oz (0.12 kg)	1 oz (28 g)	10
5 weeks	1 lb (0.45 kg)	3 oz (85 g)	6
10 weeks	2 lb (0.9 kg)	5 oz (140 g)	5
20 weeks	4 lb 4 oz (2 kg)	6 oz (170 g)	4
30 weeks	6 lb 10 oz (3 kg)	7 oz (200 g)	3
Neutered adult	9 lb (4 kg)	6½ oz (185 g)	1
Unneutered adult male	10 lb (4.5 kg)	8½ oz (240 g)	1
Pregnant female	7 lb 8 oz (3.4 kg)	8½ oz (240 g)	2–3
Lactating female	5 lb 8 oz (2.5 kg)	14 oz (400 g)	4

When to feed

Most owners feed either morning or evening, and sometimes both, depending on their cat's age, needs, or individual preference; some cats do better when fed little and often, while others are happy to eat their daily allowance in one helping. Try to encourage your pet to eat his food at a single feeding rather than leaving uneaten food out all day. Wet food, in particular, spoils rapidly, resulting in waste if your cat doesn't eat it all. You will soon get to know how much your pet will eat at one time, so you can figure the right amounts to split his daily allowance into.

Feline obesity is a common problem these days, so it's essential to restrict your pet's daily ration to the manufacturer's or your vet's guidelines on feeding. Treats

Choose cat dishes that have flat, non-slip bases and can't be tipped over easily. They should be shallow enough for the cat to eat and drink from comfortably, yet deep enough to contain food and water, and be easy to keep scrupulously clean. Suitable materials are (left to right) stainless steel, ceramic, and plastic. Discard worn or cracked bowls, as they can harbor bacteria, as well as injure your cat's mouth.

should be included in the daily ration, not given as extras. Obesity can lead to all sorts of health problems and drastically shorten your pet's life.

Water for life

Some cats dislike hard water (which contains a high concentration of mineral salts, indicated by limescale deposits in cooking utensils) and won't drink as much as they should for good health. In this case, try offering your pet filtered water or even softened water, if available. Avoid using bottled mineral water, as this also tends to be high in minerals.

Homemade food

Many cats like homemade foods, but basing an entirely balanced diet around them is very difficult. A vitamin and mineral supplement will almost certainly be necessary, so consult your vet for advice. For ease of feeding (particularly for busy owners), it's simpler to stick to commercial cat food and give an occasional homemade meal as a treat or to tempt a cat who is ill and has lost his appetite. Always allow

Top tip

Although many cats appear to enjoy eating it, chocolate can make them very ill or even prove fatal, so don't give it to them as a treat. Give them milk-drop treats instead, or chocolate drops specially formulated for dogs.

cooked foods to cool before serving. Items such as cooked cereal, rabbit, poultry, fish, and scrambled eggs are often appreciated, but be sure to remove all bones from meat or fish before feeding.

Varying the diet

It is possible to combine a homemade diet with a commercially prepared one so that your cat has the best of both worlds. A varied diet helps keep him interested, and therefore content with life, as well as helping to negate a tendency to be fussy about what he will eat.

ABOVE *Homemade food can be a treat for your cat, but remember that it may not contain the right balance of nutrients for his needs.*

LEFT *Water is essential for life, and your cat should always have access to a fresh supply. Refill the water bowl each day and scrub it regularly with clean water (don't use detergents, which can taint the bowl).*

Did you know...?

Cow's milk is very high in lactose (milk sugar), which some cats find difficult to digest and can cause diarrhea. Some cats are also allergic to the protein in cow's milk. Instead, give special "cat milk" (available from pet stores), which is lactose-reduced yet still rich in the essential calcium that cats need for strong, healthy bones and teeth.

A suitable varied diet for an average cat (a fit and healthy adult) with an average weekly energy requirement of 1,400 to 1,800 calories (5,880 to 7,560 kilojoules) can be made up in many ways. The chart below represents an example of using a variety of different foods over five weeks (plus a constant supply of drinking water). At the end of the five weeks, you can start again at Week 1.

VARYING YOUR CAT'S DIET OVER 5 WEEKS

Week	Total amounts (to be split into daily feedings)
1	7 small cans/pouches wet/semi-moist cat food plus 1 pt (600 ml) cat milk
2	1 lb (450 g) dry food plus ½ pt (300 ml) cat milk
3	2 lb (900 g) cooked rabbit meat, 8 oz (225 g) cooked liver, and ¾ pt (450 ml) cat milk
4	1 lb (450 g) beef, 1 lb (450 g) melts (spleen), 8 oz (225 g) oily fish, and ½ pt (300 ml) cat milk
5	4 cans/pouches wet/semi-moist cat food, 4 oz (112 g) dry food, 8 oz (225 g) white fish, and ¾ pt (450 ml) cat milk

FEEDING GUIDELINES

- Feed your cat in the same place and at the same time every day.
- Place a feeding mat or newspaper under bowls, as many cats like to drag their food from the dish and eat it on the floor.
- Don't disturb the cat when he is eating.
- Leave wet or semi-moist food out for at least an hour before disposing of leftovers, as most cats eat slowly.
- Introduce any changes to the diet gradually to avoid digestive upsets.
- Never give spiced food or anything to which alcohol has been added.
- To prevent choking, remove bones from fresh meats and fish.
- Always provide fresh, clean drinking water.
- Don't give your cat cow's milk; provide special cat milk or goat's milk instead.
- Keep food and water bowls clean.
- Never allow your cat to eat chocolate intended for human consumption.
- Consult your vet if your cat shows any reluctance to eat or drink.

FOOD HYGIENE GUIDELINES

- Most cats prefer their food at room temperature, so always allow refrigerated foods to warm up before serving.
- Canned foods deteriorate quickly once opened, so refrigerate and use within 24 hours. Put leftover food into ceramic, stainless steel, or plastic food containers, just as recommended for human foods.
- Place your cat's food and water bowls well away from his litter box.
- Household disinfectants and detergents can taint food and water bowls, so use salt solution (1 teaspoon to 1 pint/½ liter of water) or a commercial pet-bowl cleaner, and rinse thoroughly in clean water. Clean bowls daily, as cats are very fussy about food hygiene, and it's essential for their health.
- Wash pet-feeding utensils separately from your own.
- When feeding semi-moist food, reseal the packet tightly in order to retain freshness and prevent moisture loss until the next meal.

Counting the calories (kilojoules)

Energy is measured in units called calories (kilojoules; kJ). The number of calories a healthy cat requires equals the number of calories his body uses each day. If this balance is well maintained, the cat stays fit and healthy, and his weight remains constant. An underfed cat gradually loses weight and condition as his body draws on reserves of fat and muscle to make up for the deficiencies in his diet. Depending on her pattern of activity, a normal female cat needs 200 to 250 calories (840 to 1,050 kJ) per day, while a male needs 250 to 300 (1,050 to 1,250 kJ). Kittens need more calories in relation to their body weight because they are growing rapidly, they are more subject to heat loss, and their energy requirements are higher.

The right environment

To be mentally and physically healthy, your cat must feel safe and secure in his environment. For you to be able to enjoy your pet to the fullest, you need to be positive that you're doing all you can to keep him happy and protected from harm. Fulfilling your cat's natural needs will help keep you both contented (see the checklist).

Checklist

- ✓ safe territory
- ✓ safe, comfortable resting places
- ✓ sense of security
- ✓ personal space
- ✓ toys to satisfy the hunting instinct
- ✓ ample food and water
- ✓ acceptable social interaction

Home comforts

The "natural" cat, allowed unlimited access to the outdoors in a safe, rural environment, has perhaps the best life of all, with the freedom to explore, hunt, play, and find somewhere comfortable and warm to rest at will. However, only a small percentage of domestic cats enjoy this feline idyll; the rest have no option but to fit into their owners' lifestyles. By considering your pet's instincts and his requirements, you can make his life as natural as possible—and therefore more pleasant for you—by implementing a few simple yet highly effective alterations both to the way you care for him and to your home.

Most people who keep cats as pets want their animals to be close to them for the affection and company they provide. To make your home as appealing as possible to your pet so that he'll want to stay in it as much as possible, you must provide him with the facilities most important to him.

To a cat, the most important thing is to mark his home with his own unique smell, which he does by rubbing his cheeks (where scent glands are situated) on furniture and other items (including you!) to deposit his scent. Glands between the toes also leave a scent message as the cat scratches. Humans can't smell this scent, but other cats can and know that the territory has a feline occupant.

Surrounded by his own scent, a cat feels more secure, but overzealous housecleaning with lots of strong-smelling disinfectants, polishes, and carpet and air fresheners can keep overriding this feline scent. This may make the cat anxious, as he can't scent-recognize his territory. In turn, this can lead to more rigorous marking behavior that may involve the cat spraying urine around the house—and humans can certainly smell that!

High and mighty

You can help increase his feeling of security by providing high places where he can rest without being bothered by anyone or by another animal, or simply watch the world go by from a safe vantage point. (His chances of being attacked from above are slim but are greater at ground level.) This is why many cats like to sit on tables, kitchen work surfaces or cupboards, and the backs of armchairs. It's sensible to put any breakable items out of harm's way.

Stairs provide cats with a good opportunity to get up high if they are anxious. There they can assess any situation and either seek sanctuary upstairs or make their way back down if they decide there's no threat.

Personal space

Just as we like to have time by ourselves for a while—to relax, to be alone with our thoughts, or to sleep undisturbed to recharge our batteries—so do cats, and just as we are likely to become irritable if our personal space and time are invaded, so are cats. So the rule is to let sleeping cats lie. Because an indoor cat will soon view your house as his territory, introducing another cat at a later time may cause many problems. If you're thinking of getting two cats, it's better to get them both at the same time so they can be introduced on "neutral" ground and can establish their own territories within it.

Playtime

Cats tend to be most lively at dawn and dusk, as these half-light times are when prey is particularly vulnerable. While dusk is not usually a problem for owners, dawn can be the time when kitty wants you to get up and play with him or

Swap toys around regularly so your cat doesn't become bored with them.

Enclosing a property so a cat can't escape its confines is almost impossible, unless you build a high, solid fence with an inverted top so the cat can't climb over it. Even then it may not prove cat-proof, since they are so agile.

Feline fact

Night is not the best time to let your cat out of the house, especially in built-up areas, as car headlights can temporarily blind cats and make them more susceptible to being hit.

feed him, while you want to catch a couple more hours' sleep before going to work. If you establish routines for feeding, playtime, and "lap time," your cat will look forward to them, and his attention-seeking will become a thing of the past. To make this quality time interesting and more fulfilling for both of you, invest in a selection of toys that your pet finds entertaining. A length of string pulled along the floor for him to chase and a Ping-Pong ball for him to bat around, pounce on, and catch will do fine for starters. Homemade toys can also include cardboard boxes, paper bags, and newspaper "tents." If you want to buy toys, pet stores carry a wide variety to suit most budgets.

Interaction

Different cats require different degrees of social contact with their owners. Some are more independent and aloof than their owners wish. Cats who have a low need for social contact may learn to tolerate their owners' attention but never seem to really enjoy it, so their desire to be left alone must be appreciated and accepted. For someone who wants an openly affectionate feline companion, this can be disappointing.

Other cats actively seek out human company and show signs of distress if they don't get enough. Certain Asian breeds, such as Siamese and Burmese, are particularly popular with people who want a "lap cat," because selective breeding has resulted in a high need for contact with their owners.

Harmony outside

If your cat has access to a safe outdoor environment, he will have the best of both worlds—freedom to roam as nature intended and a warm bed and sustenance to come home to. There are several things to consider, however, if you allow your cat outdoors:

- maintaining good relations with neighbors
- your cat's safety in the yard and beyond
- preserving wildlife and birds

Keeping everyone happy

Neighbors who object to cats going into their yards to relieve themselves and/or hunt can make life pretty unpleasant for both you and your pet, so if you have such neighbors, it may be worth it to consider building a large enclosed pen with shelter to house your pet when you allow him outside. Your cat will then be safe and able to enjoy being outdoors, your neighbors will be happy, and you can relax, knowing that all is well and no neighborhood feud is likely. Keeping your cat in an outdoor run has another benefit in that he will be safe from traffic and other outdoor hazards, won't be bothered by humans or

Climbing trees

Many people are concerned when cats climb trees, but contrary to popular belief, it's rare for cats who are accustomed to being outdoors to become "stuck." They will usually find a way down safely themselves. Cats who do get stuck are either kittens or older cats who haven't had experience with climbing trees.

Always check under your car before driving off. Cats have a tendency to sit underneath stationary cars and, if they can climb in, to curl up under the hoods of parked cars for warmth.

other animals, and will be less at risk of contracting diseases from other cats.

Outdoor safety

Outdoor hazards include vehicular traffic, harassment from other animals and humans, poisoning from harmful substances, drowning in water-storage tanks, and contracting diseases from other cats.

• **Poisons** Keep garden chemicals safely locked away. When you service the car, thoroughly clean up any spilled antifreeze and oil; cats find the former appetizing and will lick it, while oil on a cat's fur or paws can result in poisoning if he ingests it while grooming himself. Most cats will instinctively avoid poisonous plants, but kittens—being interested in anything and everything—will occasionally nibble on them. If you are concerned about this danger, remove any toxic plants, if possible; your vet can advise you about which are the worst offenders. Cats can also be poisoned by eating contaminated prey animals and birds.
• **Toad poisoning** Cats do tend to catch frogs, and the occasional toad, before they know any better. Toads emit a vile-tasting and sometimes toxic substance when they're under threat. Cats react to this by shaking their heads

Harness-and-leash training

Some people like to train their indoor cats to go out for exercise on a leash. Siamese cats, in particular, don't seem to mind this, and can be trained readily, while other cats resist fiercely. It depends on the individual cat as to how successful leash training will be. Bear in mind that taking a cat for a walk is not the same as walking a dog; the cat chooses where he wants to go, and when—not you. You will need a cat harness and a light leash long enough for you to remain in contact with your pet without pulling at it. Begin training in the house, where he will feel safe and secure. Accustom him to wearing a harness first, and once he is used

to this, you can attach the leash. Don't pull or jerk the leash, but simply allow the cat to wander at will, with you following. Be prepared for leash training to take weeks, or even months.

Start early if you want to leash-train your cat; kittens take to it more readily than adult cats. Never take your leashed cat to places where he could be chased by dogs; restraining a frightened feline under these circumstances is difficult, and it could end in tragedy.

frantically, salivating, and pawing at their mouth, in an effort to rid themselves of the nasty, irritating substance. If you suspect toxic toad poisoning, consult your vet immediately.

• **Snake bites** Consult your vet immediately if you suspect your cat has been bitten by a poisonous snake.

• **Drowning** Rainwater storage tanks can prove lethal to curious cats because once they fall in, they often can't get out. Be sure the lids on such tanks are properly secured and weighted down so that they can't possibly be dislodged.

Preserving birds and other wildlife

See "Frequently asked question" on page 89 for information on this subject.

Indoor living

Living in urban environments is becoming increasingly dangerous for cats, mainly because of the continuing increase in traffic, which leaves many cats at risk of being killed or injured by passing vehicles. For this reason, many owners prefer to keep their cats inside, only allowing them outside to play, benefit from fresh air, and be entertained by watching passing wildlife in the safe confines of a pen, either freestanding or adjoining the house.

Adult cats who have been allowed regular free access to the outdoors often don't adapt easily—if at all—to living permanently indoors. Boredom can be a major problem with indoor cats, especially active types, and often leads to behavior problems. If an indoor living routine is established correctly, it is often very successful, providing you keep your pet stimulated, exercised, and entertained.

Hiding dry cat food around the house will encourage your cat to "hunt" for his food, and providing him with a

Suitable ready-made runs are often advertised in cat magazines. A concrete base to put the pen on will enable you to clean and disinfect it easily.

Indoor safety

Although you may think your home is safer for your cat than the great outdoors, there are a number of potential hazards you need to be aware of for your pet's well-being.

Many indoor cats enjoy being able to watch what's going on outside, and this helps to alleviate boredom.

• **Stoves** Cats insist on jumping onto things, and stoves are no exception. It's safer to keep your cat out of the kitchen while cooking and to make sure the stove burners have cooled down before allowing him back in.

• **Washing machines/dryers** Check these before closing the door and turning them on to be sure your cat hasn't crawled in for a nap.

• **Refrigerators/freezers** Before closing the door, check that the cat hasn't jumped in to see what goodies he can sample.

• **Cleaning fluids and detergents** Make sure your cat does not have access to these.

• **Powder carpet fresheners** Cats may suffer paw, skin, and respiratory problems from these products, so avoid them.

• **Electrical wires** These can prove fatal if chewed, but young, curious cats often view them as irresistible play items. Keep wires to a minimum in areas of the house where cats are allowed to roam.

• **Sewing materials** Keep pins, needles, thread, and buttons safely away from your pet.

• **Human medicines** Keep these in a cupboard or drawer so your cat doesn't have access to them.

• **Hot water** Keep your cat out of the bathroom while you are running a bath so he can't jump or fall into the hot water. As an extra precaution, run the cold water first and add the hot to suit afterward.

multitude of play items will help keep him occupied. Some owners even set aside a "playroom" for their cats, equipped with climbing frames, scratching posts, and a selection of toys and tunnels—even a shallow running-water feature and indoor garden containing grass and cat-friendly herbs to explore and drink from or nibble at.

Establishing specific times for play and affection will also provide your pet—and you—with something pleasant to look forward to and will help keep feline boredom and potential behavior problems at bay.

Grass and herb seed kits to create an indoor garden for your cat are available from pet stores and garden centers; indoor water features are also available.

Feline fact

Fit, healthy cats are good at righting themselves to land on all four feet when falling from a reasonable height, say 10 feet (3 meters) or so—thus saving themselves from serious injury. Sadly, they can't always do so when falling from greater heights, such as from windows or balconies in high-rise buildings.

Some indoor plants and cut flowers are poisonous to cats, so check the labels before buying. Thorny plants can result in nasty paw and eye injuries, so it's best not to have these in the house or yard. Your vet can advise you about which plants you should steer clear of.

Frequently asked question

Q What should I do if my cat gets lost?

A Cats who are allowed outside are at risk of disappearing for a number of reasons, including being hit by a car, being stolen, being accidentally shut in a neighbor's garage or shed, being mistaken as a stray and taken in by a well-meaning person or a shelter, and climbing into a delivery truck and getting out again miles from home. The pain of not knowing what has happened to your pet can be devastating. If your cat is lost, there are several courses of action to take.

• Contact local authorities to see if there have been any cats reported killed or injured on the roads.

• Contact local vets and animal shelters to see if your cat has been brought in. If your cat is microchipped or is wearing a collar and ID tag, he will be immediately identifiable.

• Ask neighbors if they have seen your cat, and if not, ask them to check their sheds, garages, and other outbuildings.

• Did a neighbor move the day your cat disappeared? Could he have "stowed away" on the moving van? You would be surprised how many do.

• Put up "Have you seen this cat?" posters in neighborhood stores, pet stores, schools, and post offices (asking their permission first), featuring a photo of your pet and a good description. Offering a reward can sometimes help bring about a speedy result.

• There is a ready black market for pedigreed cats, so if yours is a purebred, he may have been stolen; contact the police and have a description of him ready.

• Contact a lost-and-found pet service to register your loss. If you have Internet access, you can find sources there by keying "lost pet" into a search engine. Failing that, vets and shelters often have contact telephone numbers for such services.

With luck, it won't be long before you find your pet, or at least know what happened to him. When you do, inform the people you told about his disappearance so they don't continue to look for him.

Bringing your cat home

Before you bring your new pet home, you must plan for the big event so it goes smoothly and is stress-free for all concerned. Setting a date well in advance for when you will get your cat will give you time to prepare all the things you'll need, shown in the checklist.

Checklist

- ✓ spare room or pen in quiet area
- ✓ carrier
- ✓ litter box and litter
- ✓ bed and bedding
- ✓ food and bowls
- ✓ toys and scratching post
- ✓ collar and ID tag

When to pick up your cat

Wait until you have free time (or take a week off from work) before bringing your cat home so that you are around to help your new pet settle in. This is especially important if he is a kitten, as he will need more attention than an adult. Naturally, he may be confused or afraid, so your task will be to keep him company, show him where his food, water, and litter box are (and litter-train him if necessary), and introduce him to the rest of the household.

Ideally, you should set aside a spare room in which to keep the cat for a day or two while he settles down; prepare it with the essential equipment—food and water bowls, a litter box, a bed, and toys.

Make sure the rest of the family (especially children) know that the cat should be disturbed as little as possible while in this room so he can adjust to new surroundings in his own good time.

When introducing yourself and children to a cat, sit on the floor so you appear smaller and therefore less threatening to him.

A cat often hides when introduced to a new home; don't try to prevent him from doing this or haul him out of his hiding place. This is his way of making himself feel secure. He will come out when he has assessed the situation and feels it's safe to do so. Simply ignore him and quietly go about your business.

If you don't have a spare room, put a pen (with the necessary equipment inside) in the quietest area of the house and use this as a "sanctuary" for the first few days after the cat's arrival.

Pre-arrival preparations

A couple of days before you go to get the cat, take the bedding he is to use at home to the breeder (or wherever you are getting him from) so that he can use it there. The cat's own smell, or that of his mother and littermates, will transfer to the bedding and make him feel more at ease both when traveling home and once you're there. When you pick him up, it's best to take spare bedding in case the cat has an accident on the way home. Also take a little of his used litter home with you to transfer into his new litter box—again for familiarization purposes.

Buy the equipment you will need (see pages 30–37), in particular a sturdy cat carrier, since it's not safe to transport a cat unconfined. Find out from the breeder or owner what food and litter the cat is used to so you can continue to use them. Also find out how much the cat is being fed, and how often.

At the collection point, line the carrier with the bedding you left there, put the cat inside, and shut the door securely. Be sure you have all the necessary paperwork (receipt, pedigree papers, registration and ownership transfer documents, and vaccination certificate, as appropriate) before you leave for home.

Traveling home

Secure the carrier on a seat with a seat belt, in the back of a station wagon or SUV, or in the footwell on the floor. The temperature inside the car should be moderate, with

Did you know...?

Cats and kittens often urinate and/or defecate when traveling, so place the carrier on a waterproof liner inside the car. Take spare bedding and some antiseptic wipes (baby wipes are ideal) to mop up any accidents.

A pen is very useful when introducing a cat to another pet. Use for the first few days, until you are sure that each has accepted the other.

sufficient airflow so that the cat is comfortable in transit; too much heat can be fatal on long trips. Offer water in a pet drinking bottle at regular intervals if you are traveling any distance. Even if the cat protests at being in the carrier all the way home, don't let him out; you or a passenger can talk to and reassure him, which may help him to settle down.

Feline fact

It takes time for cats to get to know their territory well, which is why they are often unsettled for the first six months in a new home. Adult cats do not cope well with changes in their territory and find it difficult to adjust to a new home. It's common for felines to return to their old home rather than stay at the new one, particularly if they haven't moved far away. Kittens find it easier to adapt.

Arriving home

Transfer the cat from the carrier straight into the spare room or pen. Take a few minutes to reassure him before closing the door and leaving him undisturbed for an hour or two to settle down and get over the trauma of traveling. When you do let the cat out into the rest of the house, leave his room or pen door open so he can retreat to his sanctuary if he feels the need to. Make sure children behave quietly and gently around him—don't let them handle him too much (even though they'll want to) until he has gotten used to them and doesn't view them as a threat. Allow the cat to investigate you and his new surroundings at his leisure; feeding him will help establish a bond.

After this initial introduction, put the cat back in his sanctuary for his first night. He will be undisturbed there, and you can also sleep soundly, knowing that the cat is safe and not getting into any mischief. (See pages 78–81 for detailed information on socializing your new cat with any other animals you may have.)

Top tip

Cats naturally want to explore a new home fully. To make this safe for all concerned, cover fish tanks, remove impregnated fly strips, temporarily board over open fireplaces, put guards in front of open fires, and keep windows and doors shut.

Settling in

After keeping the cat in his room or pen for the first week (allowing him out for exercise and gradual acclimatization periods), you can allow him free access to the rest of the house. Try to feed and play with him at regular times to establish a routine that he looks forward to, which will strengthen your relationship.

Don't let him outside for the first two to three weeks, depending on his personality, or you may risk not seeing him again. Friendly, laid-back cats are likely to adjust to their new homes more quickly than timid ones. Once the cat is feeling at home, you can move his bed and litter box to their permanent positions and show him where they are. You can also gradually introduce him to wearing a collar.

Frequently asked question

Q How soon after I get a cat should I take him for a health check?

A Give the cat or kitten a couple of days to settle down, then take him to the vet to ensure he is fit and healthy and not suffering from any obvious ailments. Take him sooner if you're worried about anything. If the vet does detect any signs of serious ill health, he will help you decide what to do. (Many breeders provide health guarantees for their animals and will refund the cost or take the cat back if there's a problem. Animal shelters have varying policies about this; check your adoption agreement.) If you get a kitten at 8 weeks, you will need to take him to the vet again at 12 weeks for his first vaccination, plus another developmental check. Choose a vet as close to home as possible so you can get the cat there quickly in an emergency. At the checkup, you can ask the vet about microchipping (which may be done then) and about neutering.

Let a new cat come to you when he is ready. Don't try to force him into interaction, or you may frighten him, which may get the relationship off to a poor start. Don't try to pick him up if he clearly does not want to be held; restricting him in this way may cause him to panic and lash out in fear. See pages 92–93 for more information on handling and interacting with a new pet.

FELINE BEHAVIOR

Cats have their own unique language. If we observe them carefully, we can get a detailed picture of their body language and actions that helps us guess how they may be feeling, what they want from us, and what they need. Many cats are treated badly or inappropriately because their owners are ignorant of what their cats are telling them. By making the effort to learn what your cat is saying to you, you will understand him better and be able to give him a better life.

Body language

Cats communicate with a wide range of facial expressions, vocalizations, and body postures. Many people talk to their cats, and sometimes they seem to understand each other. Cats have a considerable universal vocabulary, and some people have tried to translate precisely what they are saying; you too can learn to recognize what your cat is communicating if you observe the points on the checklist.

Checklist
✓ watch
✓ listen
✓ learn
✓ understand

Curious

Alert and interested, this kitten is relaxed, but his body posture and facial expression (wide eyes and twitching whiskers) indicate he has seen something that is worth investigating and not considered a threat.

Friendly

With his tail up and curled in greeting and his paw raised, this cat is ready to come forward once he's sure it's safe to approach and rub against the person or other animal in an effort to make friends quickly.

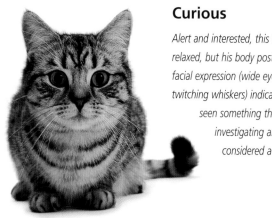

Playful

This cat is relaxed and playing.

Relaxed

With his paws tucked under him, this cat has no fear that they will be needed. His hind legs are outstretched, and he is in a vulnerable position that a tense, wary cat would not adopt. His pricked ears and wide eyes indicate that something has caught his interest.

Bored

Lethargy, alternating with bouts of almost manic behavior, is a sign of boredom and stress (it can also be a sign of physical illness).

Sleepy

Dozing and totally relaxed, lying on his side with claws extended as opposed to drawn in for protection, this cat is not ready to run. His face and ears are relaxed and the whiskers are forward. His tail is laid out, not tucked under him. All of these body signs indicate that he is comfortable and relaxed in this otherwise vulnerable position.

Anxious and worried

This cat's tail is tucked under to keep it out of harm's way. His weight is centered over the hind legs in readiness to run or strike with the front claws if necessary. His ears and whiskers are rotated to keep them out of the way in a fight, and he's looking upward for a safer place higher up. He is meowing loudly to attract a rescuer.

Uneasy or depressed

A combination of tense body posture, uneasy expression, lowered ears, drooping whiskers, and tail carried low indicate all is not well with this cat. He may be feeling unwell or out of sorts.

Feline fact

Cats soon learn to meow for attention from their owners, and they do it all the more if we leap into action and deliver what they want. They can train us very well indeed! Female cats in season also use their voices to great effect to summon mates; this is known as "calling" and is used continually until the cat has successfully mated. Males also have their own range of "love calls." Cats appear to retain their kitten vocal signals to communicate with their owners, but they use an adult repertoire of sounds with other cats.

Wary

Crouched down, back end low, tail tucked under, and poised for flight, this cat is wary about something he has sensed or seen. His face is tense and watchful, and the ears are pricked to pick up sound information.

Defensive

Faced with a potential threat, this cat flattens his ears, whiskers, and tail to keep them safe and averts his gaze so as not to antagonize the aggressor further. His paw is raised in readiness to strike if necessary. Vocalizations include growling or a low-pitched nasal yowling sound.

Frightened

This cat is trying to make himself appear small by lowering his body and angling it away from whatever is troubling him. His tail is tucked under and his ears are flattened against the head to protect them in the event of a fight. His eyes look bigger than normal as the eyelids are pulled back to allow him to take in maximum visual information. Fear response dilates the pupils. Vocal expression indicates his fear.

Aggressive

The defending cat has rolled onto his back so that all four feet can be used in defense, and he is striking out at the vulnerable face of his attacker. The aggressor has his ears pulled back out of harm's way and his eyes shut to protect them, and he's using his front paws to strike his victim. His back end is positioned and tensed to carry out the assault.

Hostile

Growling, hissing, and spitting loudly, ears back, and defensively poised to flee or fight depending on his potential foe's actions, this cat is displaying a hostile reception to whatever is approaching him.

Frequently asked question

Q Why do cats purr?

A Purring usually indicates contentment and a sense of well-being; a deep purr can also indicate pain, but if you know your cat well, you will be able to tell the difference in his demeanor. Cats start to purr at one week old and can do so continually as they inhale and exhale. Young cats purr in a monotone, while older ones do so in two or three resonant notes. All cats purr at the same frequency—25 cycles per second—but exactly how they produce the sound is still a mystery, although some scientists believe it originates in the cardiovascular system rather than in the lungs or throat.

Submissive

This kitten is crouching low to make himself as insignificant as possible and is not retaliating, yet he is poised to make a quick getaway if necessary. His ears are back to keep them out of harm's way.

Did you know...?

• Nose-to-nose greetings between cats are unusual, as it puts both in a vulnerable position. However, cats who know each other well but have been apart for a while feel safe enough to do this to confirm visual recognition and gain information about how the other cat is, where he has been, and what he's been doing.

• Cats who know each other well often play-fight. It may look and sound violent as they posture and paw at each other as in a real fight, but if you look closely, you'll see that their claws are not out and their bites are inhibited as they leap on each other, roll over, and rake with their back feet.

Attention-seeking or hungry

If this Manx cat had a tail, he would raise it in greeting. His ears are pricked, his expression is alert, and he is standing taller on his paws in an effort to get nearer to a person's face for attention, either petting or feeding. This posture is usually accompanied by the cat winding himself around legs, rubbing himself against a person, and using vocal sounds (from strident meows to "chirps") to gain his owner's ear.

Flehmen reaction

The Jacobson's organ in the roof of a cat's mouth allows him to "taste" smells. To use it, he opens his mouth a little—which looks as if he is grimacing—to draw air in for assessment. It is often used by tomcats to sense the reproductive status of females.

Stalking

This cat is completely motionless, eyes wide for maximum visual information and focusing on the prey, and ears pricked for maximum sound information on exact prey location. His back end is bunched up ready to spring, and he'll wag it from side to side immediately before he executes the pounce.

The wildcat in your home

Despite his independence, the cat has insinuated himself into the hearts and lives of many people, eventually establishing himself firmly as both a household pet and an object of acquisition as specific breeds developed. His checkered history over the centuries—from wild animal to revered pet, hunting partner to object of persecution—has contributed to the character of the cat as we know him today. The cat's main personality traits appear on the checklist.

Checklist
- ✓ independence
- ✓ self-sufficiency
- ✓ wariness
- ✓ curiosity
- ✓ watchfulness
- ✓ opportunism
- ✓ instinctiveness
- ✓ caution
- ✓ selective affection

Did you know...?

- As recently as 1964, a new species of wildcat was discovered on the tiny island of Iriomote, near Taiwan.
- Lynxes are the only wild members of the cat family to live in both the Old World (before Europeans discovered America in the fifteenth century) and the New World.

Where cats came from

Cat-like animals were in existence long before the earliest humans. The precise ancestry of cats is undetermined, but it's believed that Miacids (weasel-like mammals), which existed some 60 million years ago, were the ancestors of the family of felines as we know them today, which gradually evolved from those tiny tenacious hunters.

Modern cats

Two and a half million years ago, some 40 species of the cat family emerged from the Ice Age; only the fittest and strongest survived. About 10,000 years ago, early humans developed from their ape-like predecessors and began to grow plants for food and domesticate useful animals. One school of thought is that it was at this point that cats began to form links with humans, attracted by the mice robbing their grain stores.

The domestic cat belongs to the same species as the wildcat of Europe and Asia, whose bones, dating back some 6,000 years, have been discovered in Jericho and Cyprus (a country that had no indigenous cats at that time). It's possible that the Cyprus cats were imported by ancient

A cat's instincts tell him that finding out who else is in his territory is essential. Identifying his competitors for food and rivals for mates is vital for survival in the wild. Even in their comfortable, domesticated world, pet cats have not lost their inborn desire to do this.

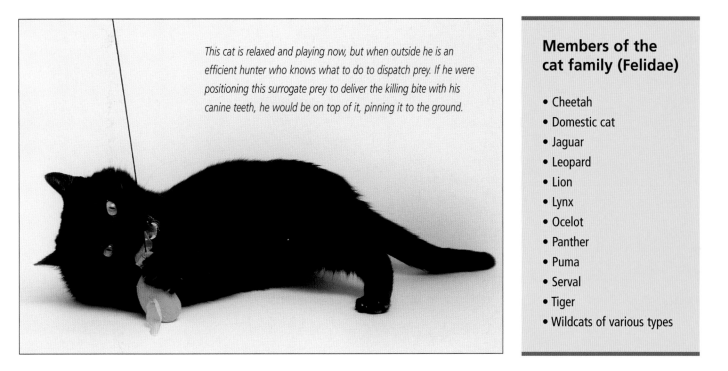

This cat is relaxed and playing now, but when outside he is an efficient hunter who knows what to do to dispatch prey. If he were positioning this surrogate prey to deliver the killing bite with his canine teeth, he would be on top of it, pinning it to the ground.

Members of the cat family (Felidae)

- Cheetah
- Domestic cat
- Jaguar
- Leopard
- Lion
- Lynx
- Ocelot
- Panther
- Puma
- Serval
- Tiger
- Wildcats of various types

Egyptians; they were almost certainly kept as pets in Egypt and were revered as sacred animals.

The first pet cats

The ancient Egyptians (from around 2,000 BC) are best known for domesticating the cat, simply because cats feature so largely in Egyptian artwork dating back to that time. As well as scenes of cats enjoying home comforts, there are also clues that cats were used to help hunt birds in the Nile delta by flushing them out of reed cover. Egyptian law not only protected cats, it also forbade anyone to take them out of Egypt; nevertheless, they were exported by traders to Greece and Britain. The Romans were also responsible for the worldwide spread of cats after conquering Egypt, having found them useful in keeping down the rodent population in army camps.

Living with man

As far as the world outside Egypt was concerned, the cat was probably an animal associated with Roman colonists and wealthy people who kept them as cosseted pets. Eventually, the cat became established on farms and homesteads within the Roman Empire, valued for his usefulness in rodent control rather than merely as a pet. The value of the cat was codified in laws enacted in AD 936 by Hywel the Good, prince of southern Wales. The law decreed that a kitten was worth one legal penny until he had opened his eyes; until he was capable of killing mice, he was worth two pence; and when he reached hunting age, his value was four pence. The law also covered the stealing and killing of cats, with the punishment for doing so severe in terms of monetary recompense to the owner.

Nowhere was the cat more highly prized than aboard ship, especially after the brown rat joined the black rat in Europe in the sixteenth century. Ships' holds often teemed with rats, and cats were the only way of keeping them under control. Ships' cats came aboard and went ashore at will, and kittens were often born at sea. In this way, cats of all shapes, sizes, and colors were carried around the world.

Feline fact

In the fifth century BC, a Persian army exploited the Egyptians' regard for the welfare of their cats. When they marched on Peluse, the Persian leader ordered his men to carry live cats in their front line as they attacked the city walls. Rather than risk killing any of the sacred animals, the Egyptians surrendered, and the Persians won a bloodless victory.

Normal behavior

What represents normal behavior in a cat is instinctive. Some feline actions and behaviors may puzzle, annoy, or distress owners, but it is important to understand that they are done for a reason—primarily so the cat feels safe and sound in his environment. No matter how tame you may think your pet is, you have to remember that he is still very much a wild animal at heart—a little lion in your midst. See the checklist for natural feline behaviors.

Checklist
- ✓ hunting
- ✓ territorial defense
- ✓ cleanliness
- ✓ alertness
- ✓ independence
- ✓ solitary habits

RIGHT *The body shape and general appearance of today's domestic cat has not changed a great deal from that of his ancestor, the African wildcat.*

ABOVE *The African wildcat is fairly tolerant of humans and can still be found living in and around villages in parts of Africa, scavenging for food as well as hunting.*

Hunting

A cat doesn't fully know how to pursue and kill prey through instinct alone; his hunting technique develops through learned behavior as a kitten by watching and imitating the actions of his mother. If a kitten has not been taught these skills, he may later catch a prey animal but not instinctively know how to kill it. To owners, the sight of a cat "playing" with his catch (repeatedly releasing and recapturing it) can be distressing, and there are several reasons why he does this.

• The cat is an inexperienced hunter and therefore a poor killer. He catches the prey but doesn't know how to finish it off.
• The cat is weakening the prey so it can't bite in self-defense when he puts his face close enough to dispatch his victim.

• He may bring half-dead prey home for his owner—viewed as a littermate—to play with and to use for practicing hunting skills, in much the same way as a mother cat would bring it home for her kittens.

Obviously, pet cats do not need to hunt for food, since their owners provide it for them, but feral cats and wildcats do— hence the need for them to retain knowledge of how to do so. Undoing millions of years of perfected evolutionary process is impossible and, apart from keeping your cat indoors or in a pen when outside, you can do little to prevent him from hunting.

Displaced hunting

Some cats have a stronger instinct to hunt than others. If they are kept indoors with no opportunity to do so, they may turn their attention to things that move in the house, targeting adults, children, and other pets. Sometimes mock chases and bites will comprise social play, and in these cases, the bites will be inhibited; in other cases, cats will display real predatory behavior and, since it's designed to catch and kill prey, considerable damage can be done to the hapless victim.

Giving the cat the opportunity to go hunting outside or to play with and "kill" toys can solve the problem. However, the fact that cats hunt and attack members of the family with whom they are usually very friendly shows how deep-rooted their hunting instinct is.

Cats often watch birds through the window and may go through some of the motions of catching them and/or chatter their teeth at them as if frustrated that they can't get to them.

Sleeping

Cats spend a large proportion of their lives asleep. As predators, they don't need to spend a lot of time eating as herbivores do, so they can afford to rest for much of the day.

Most cats hunt alone, but there have been cases of cooperative hunting by cats from the same family.

This cat is displaying displaced hunting behavior, pouncing on his owner's legs and feet as if he were a prey animal. However, in this case, the behavior is more social play than real predation, since the cat's claws remain sheathed and his bites are inhibited.

quickly realize that it's only you stroking him, but some react defensively and may scratch or bite in self-defense, much to their owners' bemusement.

Scratching

Cats are armed with razor-sharp claws that are hooked at the ends so they can get a good purchase on prey and can climb out of danger. Normally kept retracted under a flap of skin so they stay sharp, claws are extended when the cat needs to use them.

Claws grow continuously and need to be kept trimmed; periodically, the old outer casing needs to be removed to reveal the new, sharp claw underneath. Cats do this by scratching the claws down a suitable surface. They also scratch in strategic places in order to leave scent messages. In the yard, trees make good scratching sites, while indoors, the furniture tends to be a favorite target—unless the cat is supplied with and taught to use a suitable scratching post.

To conserve energy and thus reduce their need to hunt for food, cats prefer to sleep in warm, comfortable places. They like to nap rather than spend long periods of time asleep, but if relaxed enough to enter a deeper sleep, they produce the same brain wave patterns that we do when we dream. During these moments their bodies twitch as if they were running and jumping, so it's easy to conclude that they are dreaming about the day's activities, just as we do. If deprived of deep sleep over a long period of time, cats can become ill.

While asleep, a cat's hearing becomes even more acute than when he's awake, to provide warning of danger. If your cat falls asleep on your lap and then wakes suddenly as if under attack from hands moving over him, he'll probably

This scratching post is too small for the cat to use properly. Cats prefer to stretch up to full height in order to use their body weight to help drag their claws against the surface.

Did you know...?

Claws can snag in clothing, and a cat can panic if he can't get free. Gently detach the claw, holding the cat firmly as you do to prevent him from pulling away too soon and becoming even more stuck and scared.

Top tip

Keeping still is often a favorite strategy for cats faced with hostility from other cats in the household. Such hostility can compromise a cat's welfare if it prevents him from gaining access to necessary resources (food, water, litter box, sleep), so watch out for this in multi-cat households.

Inexperienced cats or kittens may climb trees or jump up to high places in panic to escape from danger, then find themselves stuck because they haven't learned how to get down. These cats are genuinely in need of rescue and may die or fall if none is available. Experienced cats simply wait for the danger to pass before climbing down.

Sitting in high places

Most members of the cat family use trees and other elevated places as vantage points; for safety, eating, and resting; and as hiding places from which to leap down and attack unsuspecting prey below. Their sharp, hooked claws help them to run up most textured, vertical surfaces. Descent from high places is more difficult, as their claws give them little support, so cats will often back down in a hopping motion (rather like bears do) before turning and leaping to the ground.

Playing

Cats play with toys (and each other, in some cases) for enjoyment and, more important, to develop their hunting and territorial defense skills or to keep them honed. Through play, kittens practice social, hunting, and fighting skills to equip them for adult life. They learn to carry small toys, or prey their mother has brought them, in their mouths and defend these from approaching siblings by growling and, if this doesn't deter them, striking out at them. As cats age, their desire to play and hunt slowly diminishes until eventually, they are content to sit around and doze for much of the time.

Urinating and defecating

When not leaving scent messages, cats like to bury their waste products so that they're undetectable. Digging a hole in which to deposit their waste and covering it up afterward ensures the area is kept clean and does not advertise their presence. Cats perform this action from an early age, as

In sibling play-fights, instinctive restraint prevents the kittens from doing serious damage to each other. Kittens are most actively involved in social play at 9 to 14 weeks; play with objects reaches its peak at about 16 weeks.

Having finished relieving himself in the hole he has dug, the cat will rake soil or litter over his waste products, then sniff at the site to check that the smell is reduced or no longer detectable. After shaking his paws to dislodge any soil or litter sticking to them, he will usually walk away from the area before settling down and cleaning himself.

soon as they leave the nest, if an easily rakeable material (soil or litter) is available. They prefer to use clean, dry material in which digging is easy, which is why sand or freshly dug earth is a favorite—much to the annoyance of gardeners and parents whose children have sandboxes.

Cats like to hide away when they are relieving themselves, and they try to find a secluded place where they will not be disturbed or vulnerable. It's important, therefore, to place litter boxes in quiet places in the house; if they're placed in busy areas, the cat may prefer to go behind furniture or in other inaccessible places instead. Being fastidious creatures, cats do not like using dirty, wet litter boxes and will often go elsewhere rather than use them, so keep the boxes as clean and dry as possible.

Scent messaging

A cat's sense of smell is very important to him, and it is highly developed. Since feline ability to communicate with body language is limited, for safety's sake, cats use scent messaging to communicate at long distances. Scent messages linger in the environment for some time, informing cats and other animals of the messenger's presence. As well as rubbing their facial and paw scent glands on surfaces, cats also use urine and feces to mark their territory.

After investigating a scent message, a cat will add his own to it. If the messenger is familiar and non-threatening, a face-rub scent is sufficient, but if a stronger message is required, the cat may choose to scratch or spray urine to cover the intruder's scent. In cases of spraying and defecation messaging, cats can discover the messenger's age, sex, state of health, and even what he ate recently.

Hygiene

Grooming fulfills many important functions in maintaining health. As well as straightening out the coat to make it a better insulator in cold weather, helping remove parasites and keeping the coat and skin healthy, grooming can also cool a cat down in hot weather by spreading saliva on the fur. Cats also lick themselves dry if they get wet, as a wet coat doesn't provide the necessary insulation. Grooming also plays a part in improving relationships between cats, with a less important cat making an effort to groom a more confident one.

Frequently asked question

Q My cat often deposits feces outside his litter box, as if he "misses" the box. Why does he do this, and how can I prevent it?

A It sounds as though the box is not big enough for the cat. Use a larger box with higher sides, and this should solve the problem. Another reason could be that much of the litter is wet or dirty; the cat will shy away from getting his paws dirty or wet and position himself on the driest part, which is usually near the edge of the box, so urine or feces is dropped over the sides. The cure is simple—clean the box out more often and be sure the litter surface is always dry.

Cats spend about one-third of their waking time grooming.

Feline fact

The back of the head and the face are the only places a cat cannot groom himself by licking, so he licks his front paws and then uses them like a washcloth to clean these areas.

Exploring

To maintain physical and mental health, it's important for cats to know their territory well. This is so they know where to find the best sources of food, where potential enemies lurk, and whether any intruders need warning off. Cats like to check their territory regularly to ensure all is well in their world, and they will rigorously investigate anything new.

Feline interaction

For cats who do not easily form friendships with others, coping with cats that are not part of their household but share their territory can be difficult. Disputes between cats over territory are common in overcrowded urban areas

where yards are small and cats numerous. One way of coping with this overcrowding is to "time-share" the facilities by leaving scent messages advertising the fact that part of the territory is temporarily occupied.

From these messages and knowledge of the other felines in the area, a cat can tell how long ago the messenger passed by, who he was, and whether it's better to proceed or to wait for a while or go in another direction. Face-to-face encounters occasionally occur, but they usually result in nothing more than lots of feline swearing and a standoff until the weaker cat backs down, since neither is usually willing to risk debilitating injury.

Hiding

Though armed with claws and teeth, cats are small, so it makes sense for them to stay out of trouble when they can. Hiding when under threat is a good strategy. Domestic cats will often run, hide, and keep still when they can't get up high or run away from danger in the close confines of a house. Shy cats like igloo-style beds in which they can curl up and hide to feel secure. This works on the principle that if you can't see them, they can't see you.

Exploring their environment vigorously enables cats to build up a detailed map inside their heads; by using this map, they are able to find new routes home, even if they have never been that way before.

Territorial behavior

The ancestors of our domestic cats did not hunt in packs but were solitary hunters who patrolled a territory that supplied them with the food they needed to survive. Although our pets are well fed by us and have no need to hunt, they have not lost the desire to stake out an area they can call their own. To them, a territory represents safety and a food supply should their humans fail to provide for them. See the checklist for what comprises an ideal territory.

Checklist

✓ safety zones
✓ vantage points
✓ abundant food
✓ water supply
✓ potential mates
✓ no adversaries
✓ resting places

Area

In an urban environment, a tomcat will opt for the largest territory he can lay claim to and defend, which may extend across several yards; in rural areas, it may cover 1 square mile (1.5 square kilometers) or more. Housecats usually treat the home as territory shared with their human household, with some core areas that are specific to themselves or others. They will accept that they are not allowed in certain places, at least if the owner of that territory is around, and may claim a particular chair or cushion as their own unless forced off it by a more dominant member of the household.

Outdoor cats lay claim to an area that they can defend from other households. This does not necessarily match human house and yard divisions and may include places not within the boundaries of their house. A new arrival who

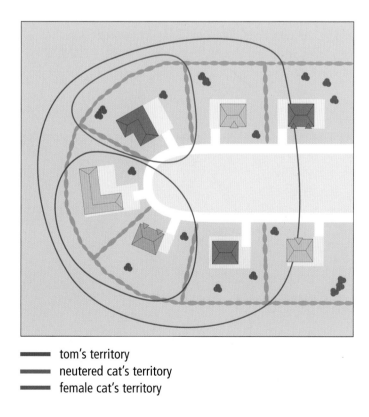

A schematic view of feline territories. Toms range over a wider area than females or neutered cats. Various factors influence territory size and, in areas with many cats, toms will evolve a network of paths.

━━━ tom's territory
━━━ neutered cat's territory
━━━ female cat's territory

This cat is marking a bush as part of his territory by spraying a small quantity of urine onto it. He is standing as tall as he can to aim the urine as high as possible, so that the message is at nose height and therefore impossible for other cats to ignore.

Feline fact

Territory is sometimes more important to cats than the family with whom they live.

finds his own backyard already claimed, and who is unable to drive off the occupant, may occupy somewhere several houses away.

In highly built-up areas where there are no yards, a cat may be reduced to an outdoor territory of little more than a rooftop or window ledge.

Marking

As well as using facial and paw scent messaging (see pages 70–71), cats often use urine as a stronger form of messaging and laying claim to territory. Males generally spray droplets of strong-smelling urine onto every convenient object along

When a face-to-face encounter happens, the cats usually deal with it by slow-motion posturing, staring, and growling until one of them backs down and moves away.

In this territorial dispute, both cats are unwilling to back down. The cat standing on the fence is in a stronger position and may be the owner of the territory, which will give him added strength. Cats can sometimes hold positions like this for hours before one finally decides to withdraw. Once this happens, the loser doesn't have a large number of signals to let the other cat know he has surrendered, so retreat must be very slow to prevent a chase and attack by the victor.

Top tip

Neutered cats' territories are much smaller than those of unneutered cats, since they are not seeking potential mates; the males do not spray and the females do not call. Territorial fights may still occur, but they will be much less of a problem, since neutered cats tend to spend more of their time at home.

the perimeters of their ranges. The tom examines a post or bush to see who has been along that way before, turns his back on it, raises his tail, and, with two or three pedaling movements of his hind legs, urinates high and accurately onto the object. Sometimes he will turn back to examine his signature or back up and rub his tail and hindquarters against the damp patch; occasionally the tom will turn and smell his mark, then scratch vigorously with his claws.

Female cats also sometimes develop the habit of spraying. Some adopt the typical male position and direct their urine backward in a fine jet.

Territorial defense

If a cat receives a threat from another cat or other animal in his territory, the following happens.

• The cat freezes and looks at the intruder; his tail lifts and starts to flick slowly from side to side. His whiskers and ears point forward, and his nose begins to quiver as he tries to identify the threat.
• As the intruder moves closer, the cat changes his stance. The point of his lifted tail turns downward, his chin is

Did you know...?

Cats are very curious about anything new appearing in their territory and will investigate it thoroughly to be sure it's not harmful or to discover whether it could be a good place to rest or hide or be useful in their continuous quest for food and hunting opportunities.

drawn in, and his ears flatten as the cat begins to turn slowly to one side. Gradually, his back arches and the hairs on his back and tail rise until he has assumed his aggressive posture.

• This menacing display continues if the intruder continues to move forward. The cat faces the enemy but turns sideways to present as large and formidable an area as possible. His hind legs become tensed and ready to spring forward in attack or away in flight. He balances on one front paw, while the other is raised, claws unsheathed, ready to strike. He bares his teeth in a snarl.

• If the unwelcome visitor backs away, the aggressor may move forward slightly, smacking his lips and salivating while continuing to growl.

• When the threat disappears, the cat sniffs the invaded ground and then marks it with his own scent.

If neither cat will give way and a fight ensues, it's often fast and furious, with a great deal of noise; each cat tries to inflict as much damage on his rival as possible with both his teeth and claws.

Fighting is usually a last resort in a territorial dispute, as close proximity to another fully armed and hostile cat is very dangerous. Toms are more likely than females or neuters to fight physically over territory.

Frequently asked question

Q My cat has stopped wanting to go out and lacks his usual *joie de vivre*. He has also begun to relieve himself around the house, which is most unlike him. Why is he doing this?

A Rogue cats who bully others can cause local cats to stop venturing out. This can lead to depression and behavior problems. Agreeing on a time-share system between neighbors for letting cats out can help. Having suffered bullying, a cat may lack confidence to go outside, so accompanying him on the first few excursions can help considerably.

Socializing

Integrating a new cat into a household is simpler if there are no other existing pets. If there are, successful socialization is possible if you go about it the right way and are prepared to be patient. The elements that a new arrival, as well as the household's existing pet(s), need for amicable integration are shown in the checklist.

Checklist

✓ adjustment period
✓ owner respect
✓ personal space
✓ privacy
✓ gradual introductions
✓ safety zones
✓ undisturbed resting places
✓ easy, unthreatened access to food, water, and litter box

Socializing with people

As has been mentioned (see pages 54–57), when you first get a cat, it's important that you let him come to you rather than force yourself upon him. This is so the cat does not feel threatened. The best way to win your cat's affection is to feed him well and make sure he has comfortable, safe, and warm places in which to rest.

Cats who have been well handled since birth and brought up in a homey, friendly, and laid-back atmosphere tend to be more sociable and easily adaptable than those who have not. The amount of socialization a kitten has with people when he is two to seven weeks old determines how well he interacts with people later in life. Good experiences in early life produce a friendly and outgoing cat.

Respecting your cat

Some cats enjoy the company of humans very much; others don't. Some cats are friendly for brief periods during the day but spend the rest on their own, doing other things. It's a case of discovering what your cat prefers and respecting

Getting to know and trust human and animal members of the household will take a while, so be prepared to let the cat approach them in his own time. Once he's satisfied that they present no threat to him, he'll begin to interact with them on his own terms. Don't try to force him into physical interaction, or he will become frightened and either keep to himself or resort to defensive aggression.

Even a small dog can look big to a kitten or cat and provoke a negative reaction, which in turn may cause the dog to chase or attack him. It's preferable to keep one of them in a pen.

that in order to build and enjoy a harmonious relationship. If you have a high need for social contact with your cat, choose a breed or type that demonstrates sociability.

Some cats stay away from humans because of a lack of trust due to poor socialization during kittenhood. These cats are timid, but they can usually be slowly encouraged to be more friendly and affectionate through patience and gentle treatment.

Children, often unintentionally, can be a great source of discomfort to cats. They can be too noisy, too rough, too active, sometimes cruel, and altogether too much for a cat to cope with. For this reason, it's important to educate your children to respect pets and treat them as they would wish to be treated themselves.

How you physically handle your cat also has great bearing on how he reacts to you. For detailed handling and interaction information, see pages 92–93.

Integration with other animals

Most cats, especially kittens, will integrate well with other animals in the household (as long as they themselves are well socialized) if given a little time. When you bring a new cat home, it may help the introduction and socialization process go smoothly if you transfer your existing pets' scent onto him. Do this by rubbing the new cat with bedding from the pets' beds or even a little soiled litter from their litter boxes before introducing them all.

Keep other pets away from the new arrival for the first hour or so, then introduce them with either one or the other safely enclosed in a pen. Don't let dogs behave excitedly or bark around the new cat, since this will frighten him and get them off to a bad start. Usually, if he is well balanced and socialized with other animals, a dog will lose interest in the new cat—especially if you provide him with a toy or treat to distract him.

Top tips

• Don't leave a new cat alone with other animals in the house until you're sure that they all get along well and are obvious friends. Kittens are most vulnerable, especially when dogs are involved.
• Keep the new cat away from pet birds or small mammals, which may be severely frightened—even if they aren't harmed directly—if he attempts to catch them. You won't be able to prevent this instinctive behavior in your cat, so the answer is to keep the animals apart.

Given time and correct introduction procedures, even the most unlikely animals can become friends.

Did you know...?

It's very rare for an adult cat to fail to accept a new kitten in the end, no matter how strong his initial reactions are. He doesn't view a kitten as a significant threat, whereas another adult represents a danger to his territorial resources.

Socializing with other cats

Introducing one cat to another may need to be a more gradual process, since cats are not naturally sociable with unfamiliar members of the same species. Always supervise the initial meetings, and never try to force cats of any age together; they will adjust to each other at their own pace. When they meet, the behavior displayed by both parties depends on several factors:

- the age of the new arrival
- the sex of the new arrival
- the personality of the new arrival
- the personality of the resident cat

When meeting for the first time, a kitten and a resident cat will probably investigate each other nose to nose (which is why, no matter what age the cats are, it's safer for one to be

It's safest to use a pen when introducing two cats; alternate which one is in the pen during several introduction sessions. The body postures of this pair show that they are still unsure of each other and need need more time to adjust.

penned so no harm can come to either). Depending on the kitten's personality he may become frightened and back away or show some bravado and even hiss; the older cat may ignore this behavior and simply sniff at the kitten, or he may become threatening—in which case, you may need to intervene. If all goes well, however, the cats will soon grow bored and tolerate each other's presence without animosity.

In one interesting case, a newly arrived female kitten simply would not take the existing cat's vocal threats and indifference for an answer. She was a confident youngster who wanted to play, and she pestered the older cat until she got what she wanted. The two eventually became firm friends. In fact, when the kitten matured and had kittens of her own, the other cat (a neutered female) took it upon herself to act as midwife and then nanny to her friend's offspring.

If the new arrival is of the opposite sex, or both cats are neutered, introductions can be easier. However, the personalities of the cats play a large part in integration, and since you can't change them, you simply have to work with and around them, taking into account each cat's needs and preferences.

This cat is totally relaxed and comfortable in his environment, so much so that he feels safe to lie in a vulnerable position while the family dog is nearby.

Give it time

Be sure that established pets get plenty of attention so they don't feel their security and status within the house are threatened by the new arrival. Having their own safe places to retreat to, undisturbed, when they feel the need, makes life easier for all concerned. It may take a week or two for the existing cat to accept the new arrival—longer if both are adults—but eventually things should settle down amicably. (See pages 82–83 for more information on introducing a second cat.)

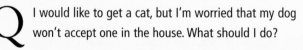

Frequently asked question

Q I would like to get a cat, but I'm worried that my dog won't accept one in the house. What should I do?

A A jealous dog can pose a real threat to a cat. If you lack control over your dog, it may not be a good idea to get a cat, since he may be put at a real risk of injury, or worse. If the dog is well trained and knows to leave things alone when commanded, you have a good chance of integrating him with a cat. If you give the dog a lot of attention normally, gradually reduce this over a period of time until he no longer expects it constantly and on demand. Once you've done this, the time may be right to get a cat.

When making the introduction, putting the cat or the dog in a pen is safest. It's important, however, not to unintentionally fuel the dog's jealousy by centering all your attention on the new cat. Giving the dog an activity toy filled with food while introductions are taking place will distract him, and he will also associate the cat with something rewarding. Doing this continually throughout the initial adjustment period should reap dividends.

Promoting health and happiness

Being a good owner means keeping your cat healthy and happy throughout his life. This entails:

• ensuring that your cat has a balanced diet appropriate to his life stage, enabling him to remain healthy
• making certain that he is vaccinated against the diseases to which he is vulnerable
• breeding your cat only if you can be certain that the resulting kittens will be normal and healthy and that they will have caring, permanent homes
• having your cat neutered if he is not going to be bred
• accommodating his normal behavior traits
• suitably addressing any abnormal behavior traits
• having the facilities and time to care for your cat properly
• taking him to the vet for checkups and if he is ill
• keeping your cat throughout his life, unless circumstances arise in which you must find him a new home (see opposite page)
• grooming your cat and attending to parasite control as appropriate
• establishing a daily routine that your cat is comfortable with; constantly changing feeding and letting-out times

Top tip

Cats feel more at ease in a home where the environment is calm and peaceful, and the unexpected does not arise very often. Animals are quick to feel tension in an atmosphere and become unsettled by it; they may react either by leaving the immediate area or, if they do not have that choice, becoming withdrawn and fearful and/or suffering ill health.

can confuse and distress a cat, which may force him to exhibit what you may consider inappropriate behavior
• always treating your cat gently and with respect and consideration
• never using physical punishment; your cat won't understand why you are treating him this way
• not relying on your cat for emotional support, as this can be detrimental to his mental and physical health
• identifying your cat's likes and dislikes

In relation to humans, cats are relatively small, and they feel vulnerable when faced with a creature bigger than themselves unless they're certain it's not a threat. For cats who have been mistreated by people, staying out of harm's way is particularly important. A friendly stare from you can often be misinterpreted by the cat as threatening behavior on your part. One of the first indications that the cat is ready for interaction is eye contact.

Did you know...?

Cats blink and narrow their eyes when they accidentally make eye contact. To make friends with an unfamiliar cat, blink and look away when you catch his eye. Even cats who know their owners well don't like being stared at. Although they get used to our eye contact when they live with us, a full-on stare can make them feel uneasy, and they will usually turn their faces away to relieve the tension. Another way they make themselves feel better is by closing their eyes. If they feel uncomfortable but not threatened enough to run away, closing their eyes lets them think "If I can't see you, you can't see me."

Finding toys that your cat likes to play with by himself will help to alleviate any boredom when you're not available to give him attention.

Cats soon get to know what time food is served and to anticipate it. Deviating from an established routine so that feeding times become haphazard can result in anxiety-related behavior.

If it doesn't work out...

It's possible that for various reasons, you may feel that your new pet does not fit into your lifestyle, despite all your efforts. If your cat is unhappy—and this can manifest itself in many ways—you and your family are probably unhappy as well. At times like this, you need to take stock of the situation. First of all, is there anything you could do, having read this book from cover to cover, that could improve it? The cat's welfare is foremost, so if there is nothing that you can implement quickly and easily, depending on your commitments, maybe you and

your cat would be better off if you found him a new home where he has a better chance of contentment.

Don't consider this a failure on your part; view it as a positive action to improve your cat's life. Rescue groups and animal shelters may be able to provide you with lots of useful information on how to go about finding the home your cat would be most comfortable with. If you decide to get another cat later, think very carefully about what type would fit well into your home situation.

Should I get a second cat?

Many owners decide to get another cat or kitten to provide their existing pet with a friend and company when they are not there. While the concept may be ideal, the reality is that the resident cat is often less than pleased with his new playmate. Being generally solitary creatures, most cats don't require a companion, so you need to ask if it's yourself you really want to indulge.

Once cats get to know and are comfortable with each other, play-fights enable them to maintain their relationship and learn about each other's abilities and strengths.

Will I be able to cope?

Before getting another cat, ask yourself the following questions. If you can answer yes to them all, you can go ahead.

- Do you have the time to help the cats integrate?
- Can you cope with the inevitable routine upheaval of integration?
- Can you afford another cat? (Think of the extra expense for food and vet bills.)
- Do you have the space and facilities for two cats?
- Do you have the time to care for two cats?
- Could you deal practically and patiently with any behavior problems that might arise?
- Do you like a challenge?

Introducing a second cat

It is true that cats provide company for each other when you aren't around to give them attention, but only once they are accustomed to

Feline facts

- Introducing a new cat to the house can cause fear and/or antisocial behavior in the resident cat. Some cats react by marking or defecating in the house, losing their appetite, deliberately breaking things such as ornaments, scratching furniture, sucking clothing, engaging in self-mutilation or obsessive grooming.
- Some breeds of cat, such as the Persian, British Shorthair, Maine Coon, and Birman, are more accepting of new cats than others.

each other. Introducing a resident cat to a newcomer is not always as easy as it sounds. Some breeds, such as Korats and Ocicats, don't tolerate other cats at all well.

Introducing another cat, or any other animal for that matter, once your pet has become established in the household can often cause more problems than it solves, whereas two cats brought up together may well become inseparable friends. This being the case, it's better to get two cats at the start, either kittens of the same age or from the same litter or two cats who have been used to living with each other. This ideal can't always be achieved, however, so it's essential to take into account normal feline behavior and learn to understand it so you will be in a more informed position to introduce another cat into the household with minimal stress to all concerned.

Cats don't live by the same code of conduct that humans do, so instead of smiling and shaking hands on first meeting, they are more likely to swear at each other and then have a fight. Since this would not start the relationship off well, it's important to follow the dos and don'ts here and avoid a bad situation.

DO:

• Follow the advice in "Socializing" on pages 76–79.

• Expect integration to take quite a while.

• Integrate the cats gradually, preferably with one in a pen to prevent either from being injured and to give them both a sense of security.

• Allow them to investigate each other at their own pace.

• When you feel they are ready to intermingle freely, wait until feeding time (when both are hungry). Choose a room that has "safe" places to which either cat can retreat if necessary, then put down bowls of tasty food, well apart from each other. Bring in the cats and close the door, then stay with them while they eat to interrupt any antagonistic behavior (dropping a big bunch of keys is a good distraction). Eating together in this way can help promote successful integration.

• Give the cats separate litter boxes.

DON'T:

• Suddenly ignore the resident cat in preference to the new arrival, otherwise the former will feel insecure, and the latter may be forced into a jealous confrontation brought on by your attention.

• Put them together and leave them to "work things out."

• Leave the cats alone together before the hissing and spitting stage has ended. Only after this is it reasonably safe to let them intermingle when you are not around.

• Expect the cats to become buddies overnight. Despite your best intentions, some cats never become great friends and only tolerate living with each other.

Top tip

Some breeds can be very people-dependent and don't like to be left alone; for this reason, it's usually better to get two kittens (not necessarily of the same breed) from the beginning to keep each other company when they're home alone. The Burmese, Balinese, Siamese, and other Asian breeds are some examples.

There may be a certain amount of spitting and hissing when cats are introduced and as they get used to each other, but providing they each have a safe area they can retire to when required, this antisocial behavior usually abates.

Behavior problems

Sometimes pet cats display what we consider to be behavior problems. To the cat, however, such behavior represents a perfectly normal action in the circumstances. It's up to us to try to understand why these problems occur and then rectify the situation so that the inappropriate behavior can be cured or redirected into an acceptable one. See the checklist for the most common triggers for behavior problems.

Checklist

- ✓ anxiety
- ✓ insecurity
- ✓ feeling threatened
- ✓ fear
- ✓ courting
- ✓ being in season
- ✓ being driven by instinct
- ✓ illness

Why cats behave strangely

In view of the constraints and relatively abnormal conditions under which pet cats live, it's surprising how few revolt against domestication or exhibit strange behavior patterns, but shock and trauma can cause problems. Rough, unkind handling can result in a totally unbalanced and unpredictable cat, and any form of severe shock may result in reactions that induce collapse of the cranial nerve and death. This can also happen to overhumanized cats on whom care and love have been lavished; here, the attack is a result of overstimulation of the nervous system.

Drugs and food additives can also cause unusual behavior in cats, so these are another area to investigate if your pet behaves abnormally. Eating a new brand of cat food or being on a course of medication can sometimes induce personality changes. Introducing a new pet or human baby to the household can cause fear in some cases and antisocial behavior in others, so you must use great care when making introductions (see pages 76–79 and 82–83).

Whatever cats do, they do it for a reason. If it doesn't suit us, we have to find ways of rechannelling the behavior so that it becomes more acceptable to us.

Feline fact

Cats can derive great pleasure from idiosyncratic behavior. Some like to play with water, particularly with dripping faucets, or to swim. Some are clever enough to use the toilet. There are cats who like snow and ice, while others won't go out in the rain. Some cats like to roll on cold concrete or paw at windowpanes. Some also cover up food they don't like, as if it were a mess in the litter box. Cats can sulk, too, by turning their backs on their owners.

Furniture scratching is a behavior trait that owners probably view as the most infuriating, yet it can be one of the simplest to prevent (see below).

Top tip

Place the scratching post in an area often used by the cat, and don't replace it when it looks ragged— that's when cats enjoy it the most, as it is comfortingly familiar and impregnated with their smell.

Scratching furniture

The arms of sofas and chairs make great scratching posts as far as a cat is concerned, while curtains are great fun to run up and hide in. He doesn't realize that this behavior is unacceptable to you. Provide your pet with alternative scratching areas and hiding places, such as:

• a sturdy scratching post, either homemade or store-bought (rub catnip on it to encourage your cat to use it); if your cat likes to climb, choose a multipurpose play/scratching post or cat "condo"
• cardboard boxes in which to hide
• lots of toys to play with
If necessary, keep your cat out of the room(s) containing prized furniture and soft furnishings to prevent from him damaging them.

Urinating or defecating in the house

It's important to identify whether the behavior is "marking" or is simply inappropriate toilet behavior. The latter may arise because:

• The cat does not like where his litter box is positioned; maybe it's too close to his feeding or sleeping area.
• The litter is unacceptable; for example, some cats won't use scented or scoopable types of litter.
• The box is too small to accommodate the cat comfortably.
• The box isn't cleaned out regularly enough.

Only a small amount of urine is sprayed when a cat marks, compared with the large volume that's expelled when cats squat to urinate.

Sometimes a cat can be encouraged to stray by kindly neighbors who make a fuss over him and/or feed him. While they may have the best intentions, it's a good idea to ask them to stop in a diplomatic way, stressing that it's for the cat's own safety and continued good health.

Sometimes a cat suddenly begns urinating outside his litter box because he has a urinary tract infection or other physical problem, so a vet checkup is a good idea. (See page 167 for more information.)

Inappropriate toilet behavior is relatively easy to cure, but marking can be more difficult, since the cause may not be readily identifiable. Marking or defecating in inappropriate places indicates that a cat feels insecure within his territory and may even feel threatened. Leaving waste in prominent places around the house is a way of marking the territory as his own and warning off perceived intruders, such as other pets or people in the household.

In one interesting case, a married owner could not understand why her previously clean cat started to mark and defecate on the bed. She later found out that her husband had been having an affair; when he moved out of the home, the marking behavior stopped and the cat reverted to using his litter box. The wife deduced that the cat was objecting to or feeling threatened by the scent of the other woman on her husband!

To help make your cat feel more secure in your home, see pages 22–23, 46–57, and 80–81.

Straying and fighting

Unneutered cats, on reaching maturity, will make every effort to escape from the house and find mates. If not allowed to do so, their frustration can lead to all sorts of behavior problems, including constant attention-seeking, house soiling, aggression, and incessant vocalization. Straying can become a real problem for owners who have unneutered male (tom) cats, while those with unneutered females may have toms hanging around the house and yard when their pets are in season. Straying can also lead to health problems caused by fighting (see pages 74–75), contracting diseases, or being injured, which can prove costly in terms of both emotional upset for the owner and the expense of veterinary treatment.

Top tips

• It's a good idea to have two litter boxes for one cat so a clean one is readily available if the other is dirty.

• Cats are fastidious and don't like to eat close to their litter box. Owners often put the food and box close together, but this can result in a real dilemma for a cat who likes to be clean. Some cats put up with it, but others take to relieving themselves in another part of the house instead.

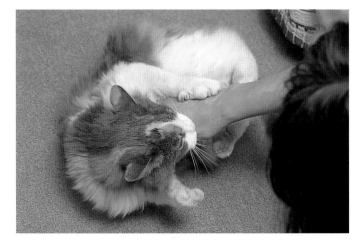

Some cats panic and react defensively when touched on sensitive parts of the body (head, underbelly, and legs). "Attack" on these areas can trigger aggressive biting and scratching to get rid of the hand. Unless you know the cat very well and he trusts you completely, it's best not to touch his vulnerable areas.

Frequently asked question

Q Why does my cat hiss at one of my children and then run away and hide?

A This is probably a result of that child tormenting the cat in some way, either physically or by loud verbal abuse, so the cat has learned to regard the child as a threat. To change the cat's perception of the child, you must teach the child how to respect the cat, handle him correctly, and move and speak softly around him. It may take considerable time for the cat to learn to trust that child, so the child should not try to handle him until the cat feels unthreatened by such interaction and will go to the child of his own volition.

Biting and scratching

Pet cats rarely become aggressive unless they are being teased or ill treated. Sometimes a cat reacts violently to being touched because he is frightened by being awakened suddenly, or he is reacting to another threat. He may be watching a menacing dog or a noisy vacuum cleaner when his owner tries to pick him up, and he thinks he is being attacked by the cause of his fear. This behavior is an

This cat's head carriage and body stance show that he is not completely committed to aggression, but hopes his hiss and posture will make the other cat back off and leave him alone.

When a cat adopts this posture and hisses, it means that he is really worried about whatever he has seen or what is approaching him. Fluffing the hairs on his body and arching his back make him bigger in an attempt to scare off the enemy.

Did you know...?

A cat who is feeling ill or is in pain may display uncharacteristic aggressive tendencies if handled or disturbed while resting; abnormal behavior like this should be checked out by a vet.

If you ignore an attention-seeking cat, he will usually get bored and find something else with which to occupy himself.

Smells familiar

In many cases of cats with indoor behavior problems, it's well worth trying a plug-in cat odor device. This works by releasing into the atmosphere synthetically produced cat pheromones, which can help settle cats and make them feel more safe and secure in a new or disrupted environment. Ask your vet about such devices, or do an Internet search.

understandable response created by the cat's complex defense mechanism.

Sexual disorders sometimes manifest themselves in unneutered pet cats when they become frustrated. Neutering usually brings about a marked improvement in behavior and general health.

Separation anxiety

Some cats—particularly certain breeds, such as the Siamese and Burmese—have a high need for contact with their owners and can become quite distressed if left alone for any length of time. This anxiety can result in various kinds of inappropriate behavior, such as destructiveness or soiling around the house and even obsessive tendencies such as self-mutilation and cloth- or wool-sucking.

Curing these habits can be difficult, since the answer lies in reducing the cat's feelings of anxiety; for example, if you are out at work all day, and the cat reacts badly to being left alone, there are a number of options.

• Impregnate a soft toy with catnip for the cat to play with and cuddle up to for a feeling of security. Some cats even respond well to a radio left on at low volume.
• Employ a pet-sitter.
• Try to work from home as much as possible.
• Find the cat a home with someone who is at home all day.
• Get another cat to keep him company.

All of these options have their drawbacks, and your circumstances and the cat's personality greatly influence which will work satisfactorily; it may be a process of elimination to find the option that works best for you and your cat.

Attention-seeking

Cats who seek attention soon learn what patterns of behavior result in their owners taking notice of them. Some knock objects over or off tables or shelves, knowing that this will bring their owners rushing to see what's wrong; others meow, rub around the owners' legs, and reach up with their paws. Reading a newspaper can result in the cat playing with it or lying on it to focus the owner's attention on the cat and not the paper.

The best way to deal with this behavior, depending on the personality of the cat, is to:

• provide him with something else to focus on, such as toys

Providing your cat with places to explore will help keep him pleasantly occupied and happy.

- move breakables out of his reach
- make the cat's environment more entertaining and therefore stimulating for him (see pages 46–52)
- get into a routine of giving your cat attention at certain times of the day that are convenient for you so he gets his quota of quality time with you, and vice versa; this will keep you both happy

Excessive grooming

Cats who are extremely bored or badly reared may indulge in excessive grooming. They lick and groom their bodies until some areas are raw and may even suck at their paws, tail, or rear nipples, purring and kneading, regressing mentally into kittenhood.

Eating or sucking cloth

This behavior (which is similar to that of a young child who sucks on a pacifier or snuggles up to a particular blanket for comfort) appears to be related to self-sucking. It sometimes occurs in otherwise well-balanced cats, especially in some types of Siamese. It is probably easiest to accept this habit and let the cat have his own piece of cloth to suck on. However, if the attraction is to man-made fibers and the cat swallows large amounts of the material, it could become impacted in the stomach and intestines and need to be surgically removed.

Top tip

Try not to allow a kitten to do things that you may not appreciate later on. For example, always feed him on the floor rather than on a table or counter if you don't want him to view such surfaces as good places to be.

Frequently asked question

Q How can I stop my cat from catching mice and birds?

A Most owners dislike their pets catching small rodents and birds, but it's impossible to stop them unless the cat is kept inside or penned while outside. You can, however, help protect birds by not allowing your cat outside at dawn (when birds are waking and off-guard in their quest for food) and dusk (when they are busy finding somewhere to roost). By limiting your cat's access to the outside at peak hunting times, his kill rate will be significantly reduced. Feed birds during the winter, when natural food is scarce, and provide them with water to drink. Position bird feeders so that they are not exposed to feline attack; put them next to trees and bushes so the birds have shelter to fly into.

At twilight and dawn, the cat's ability to make the best use of poor light conditions stands him in good stead for catching prey.

CARING FOR YOUR CAT

There are many aspects to cat care and management, and part of the attraction of owning these splendid creatures is the interaction many owners enjoy in keeping their pets healthy and happy. There is something extremely satisfying in knowing that the animal in your care is receiving meticulous attention to all his needs. For many people, the daily routine of looking after a cat, from cleaning out his litter box to making sure his coat remains tangle-free and glossy, is very fulfilling, and the purring affection received in return is blissfully comforting.

Handling

How you handle and interact with your cat will determine his behavior toward you. Cats feel threatened and insecure when there is tension in the air, when they hear loud or raised voices, when they are touched roughly, and when they are suddenly grabbed at. Cats respond better to and prefer humans who behave as shown on the checklist.

Checklist

✓ use a gentle touch
✓ are unhurried
✓ are at ease
✓ speak with a low, soft voice

Petting

If petted from an early age, most cats will be used to and enjoy it. However, there are areas of their bodies where stroking can cause them worry. If the cat was not well handled as a kitten or has been badly treated or teased, it's wise to stroke only "safe" areas—the back and sides. Avoid petting the head, where all the sense organs are, as well as the sensitive tummy and delicate legs.

Cats often enjoy being gently scratched at the base of their tails and will arch their backs in delight when you do this. Scent glands are situated in this area, and the cat appreciates any action that helps spread his own scent onto his companion. However, it's safer not to stroke this area unless you know the cat very well, as some cats may react defensively if they have had their tails pulled in the past by cruel humans, or if they have had tail injuries. If your cat scratches and bites you when you attempt to pet or hug him, see pages 84–89.

Feline fact

From the neck along the back is a "safe" area in which to stroke an unfamiliar cat. No senses or sensitive areas are located in this region, and most pet cats will tolerate being touched there. If he likes you and feels comfortable, the cat may then invite you to stroke his head by trying to rub his face and body against your hand.

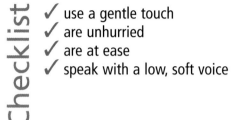

This cat's body language says that he does not appreciate being held: He's pulling away from the child's face and looks concerned. Attempts to make a cat like you by picking him up and holding him, when he would not stay with you if he were free, are likely to fail.

Frequently asked question

Q When should I start handling kittens?

A Handle them frequently between the ages of three and eight weeks to get them used to people. This is the time for kittens to recognize the difference between safety and danger. Start gentle grooming at this age, especially in longhaired cats, with particular emphasis given to inspecting ears and mouths. Training at this stage is invaluable.

Picking up your cat

The best way to pick up your kitten or cat is shown here. Gently scoop him up with one hand under his chest and the other supporting his bottom, keeping him close to your body so he feels secure. Don't hold him too tight, or he'll become claustrophobic and try to escape.

Carry the cat with your hand underneath his chest and your fingers between his forelegs, keeping him close to your body for support. This leaves one hand free to hold the cat's head or gently restrain him by the scruff (the loose skin on the back of the neck) if necessary.

Some people find it easier to hold a cat across his midriff, with one hand cradling the cat and the other held lightly across the length of his back for security (some cats also prefer this method of holding and carrying).

Your cat's expression can tell you a lot about how he is feeling. Apprehension and worry show in this cat's face. His ears have swiveled back to find out what's going on behind him and are held slightly back, indicating his concern. Being held, he has little control of what happens to him; he can't run away, and this makes his fear worse. If you are holding your cat and he displays similar behavior, set him down gently; otherwise, you may be scratched or bitten, and your cat may avoid being held in the future.

Top tips

• A kitten who has had at least four kind and gentle handlers during his early weeks will be relaxed and friendly with most people.

• To accustom a cat to being picked up and held, start by doing this when you are seated. Pick him up and hold him for only a brief time at first, then put him down again. Gradually extend the time you hold him until he is content to remain in your arms as long as you are giving him attention, but always allow him to get down if he wants to.

• Since cats are equipped with sharp teeth and claws, it is sensible not to antagonize them during interaction. If you are susceptible to cat-scratch fever—a severe response to infection caused by cat scratches and bites, also called cat-scratch disease (CSD)—take precautions when handling your cat and wear gloves and long-sleeved clothing.

Cats and children

Research has shown that children who grow up with pets in the house and are taught to treat them with respect and care are more likely to develop into well-balanced and responsible adults. What better reason could there be to have a cat if you are a parent? To create harmony between children and a cat, you should observe the rules in the checklist.

Checklist

✓ supervise interaction
✓ teach children to respect the cat
✓ demonstrate correct handling procedures
✓ encourage bonding
✓ involve children in daily care
✓ forbid cruelty

How cats react to children

It's surprising just how tolerant some cats and kittens can be with babies and young children, but this is not something you should put to the test. You must teach children not to disturb the cat—especially by grabbing at him—when he is resting in his bed, or they may be rewarded with a scratch. Your cat may sleep for up to two-thirds of the day, which is quite normal.

Feline fact

Cats who have been well socialized with humans during kittenhood and are treated in a way that makes them content will successfully fulfill the role of companion and even of child substitute for childless couples.

Interaction

Discourage young children from impulsively picking up a kitten or cat, because they may squeeze too hard around the abdomen and make the cat resist being carried. Instead, encourage the cat to climb onto the child's lap and remain there to be petted. Demonstrate how to stroke the cat and the correct way to pick him up and carry him (see page 93). The cat should never be restrained during these encounters; make sure that the child understands that she must allow the cat to walk away whenever he wishes.

Prevent all children, especially toddlers, from chasing the cat, as this can make him avoid young children for life.

Similarly, the cat should be able to rest undisturbed without being pestered, as nervousness and fearful or unpredictable behavior are fueled by lack of sleep. Provide plenty of areas to which cats can escape from children's attentions—high places are preferable so your pet can seek sanctuary when it all gets too much for him.

If initial interaction between children and cats is done correctly, they usually become great friends. Many cats and kittens bond quickly with children and seem happy to play with them, curl up with them to sleep or watch TV, and "help" them with their homework.

Frequently asked question

Q How can I prepare my cat for the arrival of my new baby?

A Cats and babies seem to have generated more urban myths than any other combination of animal and human. Some health professionals seem intent on perpetuating tales of woe surrounding pets and a new addition to the family, but common sense is all that's required. If your cat is used to a lot of attention from you, bear in mind that you may not be able to devote as much time to him when your baby arrives. Gradually wean your cat from being so dependent on you; get into the habit of setting aside a convenient time of day to spend time with your pet, sharing affection and playing with him. Once your cat gets used to this, he should be happy to accept it. Giving your pet other things to focus on, such as some new toys, will also help reduce his dependency on you for attention and entertainment.

Get the cat used to seeing baby equipment in the house, and seeing you fussing around it. When you have the baby, use a clean cloth to transfer her scent onto your cat, his bedding, and household furniture and surfaces. This will make the baby's arrival less of a surprise to the cat. Be sure to let the cat greet the new arrival and "help" you attend to her; handling the situation calmly will help the integration process go smoothly.

Children can sometimes find it hard to express their feelings to parents—or anyone else, for that matter. A cat will not judge or admonish them and therefore can be a source of great solace and friendship.

To cats, children are not the same as adult humans; they move, talk, and even smell different. If the two are integrated correctly, they will get along just fine.

Did you know...?

A common misconception is that a cat may try to sleep in a baby's crib or carriage and smother the child, but this is highly unlikely. However, to put your mind at ease, it's sensible to use a special net (available at most stores that sell baby furniture) as a precaution and to keep your cat out of the room in which your baby sleeps.

Hygiene

Young children especially tend to put their hands in their mouths at every opportunity, so while it's rare that a child will pick up any infection (such as ringworm, tapeworm, or toxoplasmosis) from felines, it goes without saying that you should make sure that children always wash their hands after handling a cat (or other animals) to minimize any risk. This is especially important if you have a yard that both cats and children like to use, since cats relieve themselves in flowerbeds and, if they get the chance, in sandboxes—exactly where children like to play. Always keep sandboxes covered when not in use to keep cats from using them as litter boxes.

Toxoplasmosis

Contracting toxoplasmosis can be a great concern to expectant mothers and parents with young children. Most infections are harmless if the person has sufficient immunity to them, but unborn and young children are at high risk.

Toxoplasma gondii is a microscopic parasite that can cause abnormalities and blindness in a fetus. Cats become infected by eating raw meat (prey), and the eggs (contained in cysts) from the parasite are shed in the feces. These eggs hatch into larvae, and it's these that can cause the damage if ingested by humans. (The parasite is also found in raw meat—primarily pork and chicken—in the human food chain, but it is usually destroyed by cooking.)

Some doctors and midwives can be overzealous in advising pregnant women to get rid of any cats in the house to eliminate any risk of contracting the disease. This really isn't necessary if you follow hygiene rules and wear gloves when handling cats, cleaning litter boxes (consider having someone else do it), and handling garden soil. The risk of humans contracting toxoplasmosis is said to be greatest when handling raw meat or vegetables grown in contaminated soil or eating undercooked meat, so this puts the chances of contracting it from your cat into context.

If you're concerned about the risks, ask your doctor to do a blood test to show whether you are immune to the infection; if you are, this means there is no risk of passing it on to your baby. If you are not immune, make stringent hygiene in your kitchen and around your cat a priority. Having your cat wormed regularly is also good practice to keep the risk of contracting toxoplasmosis to a minimum.

Cats and children can have great fun together, providing the latter are taught to know when to leave the cat alone.

Feline fact

Cats don't understand if you punish them for digging their claws in when you pet them; with children, it's wise to place a thick blanket over their knees when they are petting a cat to prevent discomfort. The occasional scratch or bite is part of owning a cat, however, so be sure that your cat is up to date on his vaccinations and that you and your family are immunized against tetanus (and rabies, if possible).

Routine care

Cats look after themselves, don't they? Yes, to a certain extent they do, but for domestic pets to live happy, fulfilled, and healthy lives, they do need some help from their owners. In order to maintain your cat's mental and physical health, there are certain things you must do on a daily, monthly, and yearly basis, shown in the checklist.

Checklist

✓ provide correct nutrition (food and water)
✓ maintain grooming
✓ give appropriate training
✓ monitor behavior, elimination and general appearance
✓ initiate stimulating activities
✓ check vital signs (pulse, respiration, temperature)
✓ control parasites
✓ provide vaccinations

Weight

Pet cats can become obese if they don't get enough exercise in relation to how much they eat on a daily basis. Being overweight can result in serious health problems and shorten the cat's life. Depending on the breed or type, the average cat weighs about 8¾ pounds (4 kilograms), and you should be able to feel his ribs but not see them. Any deviation from normal weight may indicate a health problem. (Longhaired cats may look fat, but it can be an optical illusion created by all that fur.)

Collars

If your cat wears a collar, check its fit daily to be sure it's not too tight and isn't rubbing or causing allergic skin reactions (in the case of flea collars). Kittens grow rapidly, so it is especially important to check the fit of their collars at least once a week.

Monitor your cat's elimination habits daily. Loose stools can indicate a problem, as can either too frequent or infrequent urination. If unusual habits last for more than a day or so, seek veterinary advice.

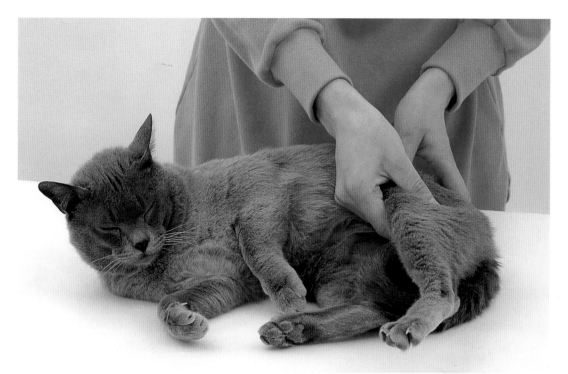

One of the best ways to take a cat's pulse is by placing two fingers on the inside of his thigh.

Elimination

The most important signs of a potential problem are:

• discomfort when urinating and/or defecating
• a constant need to eliminate (shown by the cat frequenting his litter box, often with no satisfactory result)
• blood in feces or urine or other abnormalities, such as loose or very hard stools
• fewer eliminations than usual
• any other deviation from usual elimination; you should closely monitor this, and if it persists for more than a day or so, seek veterinary advice

General demeanor

If you know your cat well, you will soon notice any difference in his behavior and demeanor. If he is normally bright and active but suddenly appears depressed, this may indicate that he is feeling ill. If there are other signs of illness, it's wise to take him to the vet for a checkup. Make a note of symptoms to help the vet work out what is wrong. If your cat deviates from his usual eating habits, this also warrants investigation. He simply may not appreciate a change of food or, more seriously, he may have a mouth ailment, such as an abscess, or a digestive disorder that is affecting his appetite.

Training

Be sure to maintain rules about what the cat can and can't do on a daily basis, so you don't confuse him. If, for example, you don't allow him to scratch furniture, don't dangle toys over the arm of a chair. This may lead him to dig his claws into the material, which in turn may encourage him to scratch. If you don't usually allow the cat on the bed, don't be tempted to let him come up "as a special treat" one

Feline fact

A cat's vital signs—temperature, pulse, and respiration (TPR) —vary depending on his age and the time of year; in hot weather, for example, they will be higher than usual. Find out what your cat's vital signs are by taking them over a period of a week (in summer and winter) to discover his average during warm and cold seasons. As a guide, feline vital signs are:

• **Temperature:** 100–102°F (38–39°C)
• **Pulse:** 160–240 beats per minute, depending on the age of the cat (the younger he is, the faster the heartbeat)
• **Respiration:** 20–30 breaths per minute

Top tip

Being fastidious creatures, cats dislike eating from dirty bowls. After each meal, throw away uneaten wet food and wash out the bowl. If you heap fresh food on top of leftover food, the cat will probably not eat it.

Cats normally spend a lot of time grooming. If your cat fails to stick to his usual hygiene routine, it may be a sign that all is not well, so take him for a checkup.

day, or he will then think he is allowed to do it all the time. Make sure the rest of the family also adheres to these rules.

Special occasions

At holidays and other festive times, be very careful that your cat doesn't become stressed with all the noise and extra people in the house or ill from eating anything unsuitable. Christmas trees, for example, can prove irresistible to curious cats, so make sure your tree is well secured in its stand, lights are plugged into a circuit breaker, and ornaments are shatterproof. Some cats are fascinated by tinsel; if your pet persists in trying to eat it, you will have no option but to remove it from the tree.

Keep the cat separated from any celebrations by settling him in a quiet room with a warm bed, some toys to keep him occupied, his litter box, and food and water; go in to check on him from time to time to reassure him that you are around. Even though you may be tempted to, don't give your pet foods that he does not normally receive, or he may suffer unpleasant and painful digestive upsets.

The use of fireworks seems to be on the increase, and most animals are terrified of them; if they're going off in the neighborhood, keep your cat safely indoors. Having the TV or radio on can help drown out the noise. If you plan to host a fireworks party, keep the cat inside, preferably in a room on the other side of the house, and choose "silent" fireworks if they're available where you live. It's also courteous to inform your neighbors of a forthcoming fireworks party so they can also keep their pets inside.

Did you know...?

Cats rapidly learn that certain kinds of behavior result in a reward, such as being fed or let outdoors. These behaviors can then become signals that they display when they want something. It is possible, for example, to train cats to sit on command, using plenty of high-value rewards, such as food morsels. On the other hand, getting cross or saying no to discourage unwanted behavior rarely works, and cats can become resentful and fearful if such tactics are used.

AT-A-GLANCE MAINTENANCE CHECKS

FREQUENCY	WHAT TO DO	FREQUENCY	WHAT TO DO
Daily	• Clean food and water bowls • Feed and supply fresh water • Check eating habits • Clean out litter boxes and check for anything unusual • Give your cat some quality time—attention and play • Be sure your cat is warm enough, depending on his age and the time of year • Groom longhaired cats • Check collar fit • Check body, legs, and paws for signs of injury	**Every two months**	• Do parasite control for indoor cats (do this monthly if you also have a dog who goes outside) • Check and clean teeth (see pages 134–35 and 164–65)
Weekly	• Groom shorthaired cats • Check ears • Check vital signs in elderly cats (see "Feline fact" on page 99) • Check litter and food supplies for coming week • Wash and disinfect litter boxes; replace litter • Check for weight loss or gain	**Every six months**	• If you choose injections to control fleas, they need to be administered every six months • Have veterinary checkup for elderly cats • Get vaccination boosters for outdoor cats in highly feline-populated areas (see pages 138–39)
Monthly	• Worm and deflea cats who have access to outside (see page 138) • Check general health and vital signs	**Once a year**	• Have veterinary checkup (see page 137–38) • Review nutrition needs depending on your cat's age (ask your vet for advice if necessary) • Get yearly vaccination boosters for indoor cats

If you take the time to learn what represents normal behavior for your cat, you will soon be able to tell when he is feeling ill, or is displaying signs that something is not right and requires investigation.

Kitten care

You need to put in some work for that cute kitten to grow up into the perfect pet. It's not hard to do this—common sense, inclination and the will to apply certain principles and procedures to training your young cat how to behave as you wish will earn rewards. All you need for basic kitten care is shown in the checklist.

✓ patience, kindness, and gentleness
✓ understanding of feline behavior
✓ appropriate veterinary attention
✓ consistent training
✓ rules that are enforced
✓ correct handling
✓ quality time together
✓ rewards for appropriate behavior

Sleeping

Cats sleep for up to 60 percent of their lives. They spend a larger proportion of their time asleep when they are kittens and again when they reach old age. It's normal for kittens to sleep a great deal; because of their bursts of frenetic play, during which they use a lot of energy, they need to replenish their energy levels frequently by resting. It is essential that kittens be allowed to rest undisturbed when they wish, to make sure they have the necessary energy to develop into healthy, well-adjusted adults.

Feeding

Kittens play hard and grow fast, and they require appropriate nutrition to cope with these demands on their bodies. Luckily for owners, manufacturers make this easy by providing a vast range of foods especially formulated for young cats. Choose food for the appropriate life stage to be sure you're fulfilling your pet's nutritional needs. See pages 38–45 for further information on feeding kittens.

Good early interaction between kittens and children provides an excellent basis for a lifelong affection for each other. Children who love and respect cats are likely to develop into adults who care about the welfare of all animals.

Handling your kitten

The way you physically interact with your kitten will greatly influence how he reacts to you and other people when he matures. The better you handle your pet as a kitten, the better he will accept physical contact as an adult. For this reason, aim to give your kitten an all-over check at least once a week, but preferably every day.

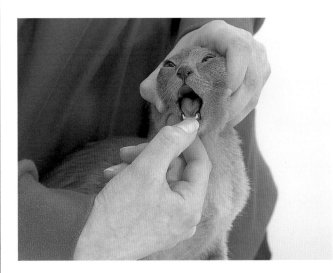

Getting your kitten used to regular inspections of his mouth will reap dividends when you clean his teeth and check his mouth later on; your vet will also appreciate this training. In addition, it will make it easier for you to administer medicines orally if necessary.

If your kitten is used to being handled all over, veterinary examinations will be less stressful.

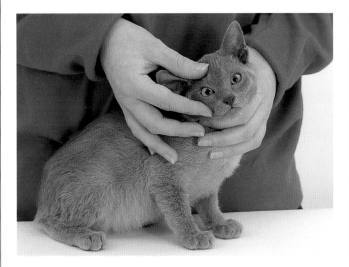

The head is a sensitive area, so the earlier a kitten becomes used to someone touching and examining his head, the easier it will be for him to tolerate this handling later on.

The ears are also sensitive, so you should handle them accordingly. Getting your kitten used to ear inspections will make treating any future ear problems much easier.

Teaching your kitten his name is easy. Simply call the name whenever you feed him, and he will soon learn through this reward-based training to respond to his name.

Top tip

Before you bring your kitten home, ask the breeder or owner for a diet sheet so that you can buy the same food items. The diet sheet should also include details of mealtimes and how much food to give. This will reduce the risk of overfeeding your kitten or supplying too rich a menu, either of which could lead to digestive upsets.

Juvenile behavior

After sleeping and eating, playing rates high in a kitten's priorities. He will amuse himself for hours with a selection of toys. These don't have to be expensive, store-bought items for your kitten to have maximum fun: Ping-Pong balls, cardboard tubes. and old soft toys will do the job just as well. Make sure, though, that none of the items can break or come apart easily, as inquisitive kittens will soon chew off and swallow a teddy bear's button eyes or a dangling string, which could result in a digestive problem requiring veterinary attention or even surgery.

You can both enjoy hours of amusement if you simply drag a length of string along the ground for your kitten to chase, pounce on, and "kill." Never leave balls of yarn or lengths of string unattended with a kitten, however, for the reasons given above.

Fishing rod–style toys should also be used only when you are there to supervise the playtime; cats who have unattended access to such toys are at risk of strangling themselves with the "fishing line."

Praise, reward, and punishment

Cats love praise and appreciate rewards, but they don't understand punishment as humans do and can't respond to physical or verbal reprimands in the same way that humans might. For this reason, you must praise and reward any desired behavior. Your kitten will soon learn that certain behavior produces good things and will strive to attain these, whereas other types of behavior produce no satisfactory response on your part and are unrewarding for him. If your kitten displays any kind of undesired behavior, try to convert it into something more desirable (see pages 84–89).

Never physically reprimand your kitten, as it won't do any good; it will only frighten him and alienate him from you. Remember that building trust takes time, but destroying it can take only a second of inappropriate response on your part.

Behavior training

Instilling desired behavior traits in a kitten will usually result in a sociable and well-behaved cat, bearing in mind the praise, reward, and punishment ideals described above. But think ahead—behavior you may find acceptable in a kitten may not be quite as desirable in an adult cat, yet the cat won't understand why you have changed your response. If you don't wish your cat to sleep on your bed as an adult, for example, don't let him do so as a kitten and come to expect this as the norm; denying him access to your bed later on may result in behavior problems.

For many owners, training a kitten to perform a range of basic, acceptable actions by means of kind, gentle, and effective methods is mutually rewarding. It really does help to be open to the feline view of the world so you can communicate effectively (see pages 58–89).

Litter training

Usually, a kitten will be litter-trained when he's ready for a new home. However, once there, you will need to show him where his new toilet facilities are. Try to use the same type of box and litter as he had in his previous home so the change will not be too radical; cats are creatures of habit. Bringing some of the kitten's used litter home with you and placing it in his new box may help him adjust to his new facilities.

Young cats are vulnerable outside, so don't let them out unaccompanied until they are well grown and have familiarized themselves with the yard and surrounding area, with you nearby to keep them out of mischief.

Environment and safety

Being naturally bold and curious—the world inside and outside the home is one big, exciting playground to them—kittens can get into all sorts of trouble and distress if left to their own devices. See pages 46–53 and 76–79 for information on keeping your kitten or cat safe.

Going outside

After being indoors for a few weeks, your kitten will be self-confident enough to venture outside. While he is small (and only when his course of vaccinations has been completed), you should let him out only when you are around to supervise until he gets used to his outdoor environment and is able to find his way around the yard and back into the house. This is the ideal time to introduce him to a cat flap (see "Frequently asked question" on page 108).

Kittens are at risk from adult cats in the area, as well as dogs and other hazards, including traffic. Being cute, kittens are also much more likely to be picked up and taken home by well-meaning people who see them all alone and

Did you know...?

• Friendly feline mothers are likely to produce sociable kittens, because they show their offspring that there is nothing to be afraid of.
• The genes a kitten inherits from his father determine how friendly he will become. His mother's genes also play a part, but the effect is not as strong.

think they have been abandoned. This is why it is so important that young cats be supervised outside until they become "streetwise."

Vaccinations

For a multitude of reasons, some people are in favor of vaccinating cats, while others are against it (the frequency of booster shots being a particular bone of contention). On balance—particularly from the veterinary point of view and in the absence of scientific evidence to prove otherwise—vaccinations are to be recommended against the nasty, often lethal diseases that cats can fall victim to. If you're considering purchasing health insurance for your pet, be aware that some insurance companies insist that cats be vaccinated before they will issue policies; if vaccinations are not kept up to date, the insurers may not pay out in the event of a claim. Check the policy terms before signing up. (See pages 138–139 for further information regarding vaccinations.)

Visiting the vet

Take your kitten for regular checkups so the vet can monitor his development and catch any potential problems early, and so your kitten becomes accustomed to going to the clinic and isn't frightened by the experience. Many vets like to see

Two kittens can provide great companionship and entertainment for each other. Play-fighting may sometimes look—and sound—alarming to the owner, but kittens rarely injure each other. This is all part of learning to assess other cats' strengths and weaknesses so they're able to defend themselves against feline intruders and other outside aggressors if necessary.

Veterinary health checks

Checking your kitten's body condition will tell your vet if he's developing normally and is in good shape physically.

A full veterinary examination will involve a number of basic tests, including using a stethoscope to listen to your kitten's heartbeat (see "Feline fact" on page 99 for vital signs readings).

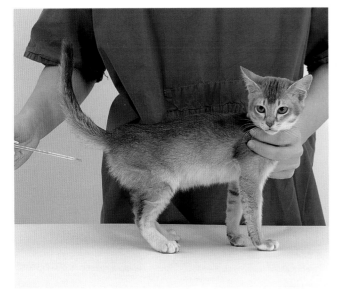
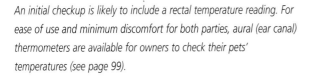

An initial checkup is likely to include a rectal temperature reading. For ease of use and minimum discomfort for both parties, aural (ear canal) thermometers are available for owners to check their pets' temperatures (see page 99).

Your kitten will lose his milk teeth at the age of about five months. Your vet will be able to tell if teething is occurring correctly and, if not, will recommend appropriate treatment.

Accustom your kitten to having his teeth cleaned from the start so he comes to view it as a normal process. Trying to clean an older cat's teeth if he isn't used to it is extremely difficult, and often impossible. (See "Brushing teeth" on page 115 for more information on this subject.)

their young patients just for a cursory exam and a cuddle so the animal doesn't view their interaction as always being unpleasant.

Worming

Internal parasites can cause all sorts of problems, including death, so it pays to consult your vet regarding a worming program for your kitten. A typical regimen is to worm kittens aged 4 to 16 weeks every 2 weeks with an appropriate roundworm product. After 6 months of age, your kitten will require worming every 2 to 6 months, depending on his lifestyle, for roundworms and tapeworms. Consult your vet for advice. (See page 138 for more information.)

Flea control

If your kitten enjoys an outdoor lifestyle or comes into contact with other cats or dogs who do, he will almost certainly require defleaing on a regular basis. Fleas can

Frequently asked question

Q What is the best way to teach my kitten to use a cat flap?

A Once your kitten knows his name and is used to going outside under your supervision, you can introduce him to a cat flap. Some self-confident kittens quickly learn that access to the inside or outside is achieved by pushing against the flap, but others may need a little more encouragement. In the latter case, kittens tend to be quite food-motivated, so a little bribery can have the desired effect. Simply encouraging the kitten to go through the flap (which can be taped open at first if necessary) by offering a tasty morsel of his favorite food will usually do the trick. Take it one step at a time and continue at your kitten's pace. Don't try to hurry your pet, because this will probably have the opposite effect. Never try to push your kitten through the cat flap in an attempt to show him what to do; this may frighten him so much that he may never use the flap.

cause all manner of unpleasant ailments, including anemia and flea allergic dermatitis, and can be a problem all year round if not kept under control. Your vet is the best person to ask regarding a suitable flea-control product for your kitten. (See page 138 for more information on fleas and how to control them.)

Trimming claws

Unlike outdoor cats, who are able to keep their claws worn to a reasonable length naturally, cats who are kept indoors may need a bit of help to ensure their claws remain in good condition and don't get too long. It's easier to get kittens used to having their claws trimmed than it is to start the procedure with older cats. Ideally, claw clipping should be done by an expert. If you do opt to do it yourself, however, ask a vet, a breeder, or a professional cat groomer to show you how to do it correctly.

Trimming the ends of the claws doesn't hurt, as long as the nail bed or quick (the thin vein that runs down the nail, which you can usually see) isn't nicked; if it is, the nail will bleed and be quite painful. If you catch the quick, the cat is unlikely ever to put up with having his claws clipped again.

Providing your kitten with a good-quality wooden scratching post (complete with bark if you can find one, perhaps even a tree branch from the yard) will help avoid the need to trim claws.

In the United States and Canada (but not Australia, where it's considered inhumane), it's legal for veterinarians to declaw cats, although some vets won't do it for ethical reasons. Some owners prefer to have their cats' front claws removed so they can't damage furniture or scratch people; declawing all four paws is rarely justifiable and is usually strongly discouraged.

Guillotine-style claw clippers designed for animal use are the best instrument for trimming claws.

Top tip

Claw clippers must be sharp, and the scissor action must be springy. Always clean them after use with clipper oil and wipe them dry. Keep them in a dry place so they don't rust and become blunt, and resharpen them or replace the blade as necessary.

Grooming

Grooming is an integral part of cat ownership. As well as helping to keep your pet's coat in good condition, carefully and gently grooming him also helps you to bond. Depending on the coat type of your cat, you will need the right tools for the job, including some or all of the items on the checklist.

Checklist

✓ blunt-ended comb
✓ fine-toothed (flea) comb
✓ wide-toothed comb
✓ de-matting tool
✓ grooming mitten
✓ soft-bristled brush (for sparse-coated cats)
✓ bristle brush
✓ slicker brush
✓ toothbrush and cat toothpaste
✓ cotton balls
✓ guillotine-style claw clippers
✓ fine blunt-tipped scissors
✓ cat shampoo
✓ silk, velvet, or chamois leather grooming pad
✓ grooming powder
✓ box for grooming equipment

Feline fact

Cats get stiffer and less flexible as they get older; seniors often need help to clean the back of their neck and the backs of their hind legs, as they find these areas hard to reach when grooming themselves.

*A wide selection of grooming tools is available for many coat lengths, thicknesses, and conditions. Clockwise from top: **rubber grooming pads**, used to gently and thoroughly groom short coats while massaging the skin and removing dead hair; **de-matting tool**, used for slicing through knotted coats (avoid overzealous use); **combs** with differing tooth lengths for various coats (particularly useful for longhaired bellies, under chins, and between the legs, but be careful not to pull the skin); **slicker brush** with slender, angled steel bristles, used for all coat types (be careful not to snag or pull the skin); and **steel/bristle brush**, used for all coat types (the bristled side is especially good for heads and tails).*

Why groom?

Cats spend much of their waking time grooming, and most are able to do a good job of keeping themselves clean without much help from us. However, longhaired, infirm, arthritic, and injured cats do need their owners to groom them to keep their coats in top condition and so help them remain mentally and physically healthy.

Long, thick hair—especially the fluffy, soft type found in Persians—will become tangled and then form dense mats if not brushed on a regular basis. Grooming a badly matted coat would be far too uncomfortable for the cat, so the only alternative is to cut out the matted parts or, in severe cases, have the coat clipped off by a vet. Longhairs can also get clumps of litter stuck between their toes, so always check for this when grooming and gently tease (or carefully cut) out any mats.

Regular grooming also reduces the amount of shed hair in the house, which is especially troublesome for owners who have allergies.

When grooming, part the fur so you can see down to the roots and check for signs of ticks (shown here) and fleas—either actual fleas or traces of their feces. Grooming is also a good opportunity to check the cat all over for any unusual lumps and skin ailments.

Hairballs

A hairball (or furball) is an accumulation of hair in the cat's stomach that occurs as a direct result of grooming himself. A solid mass of hair forms and rubs against the lining of the stomach; this irritation prompts the cat to vomit the hairball. If the hairball lodges farther down the digestive tract, it may cause a blockage; the cat may show signs of decreased appetite, constipation, and general lethargy. Seek veterinary attention if you suspect a blockage. Grooming your cat regularly will help prevent these problems.

All cats produce hairballs, but longhaired types tend to suffer more due to the quantity of hair they ingest while grooming themselves. The cat's tongue has a rough surface with a series of backward-facing spines that act like a comb to remove loose hair, which the cat then swallows. Cats will often eat grass, which acts as an emetic, to help them vomit hairballs.

Step-by-step grooming guide for long coats

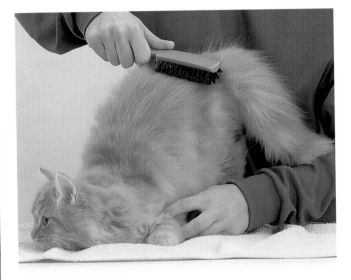

1 *Do the back first: brush in the direction the hair is lying, working backward from head to tail. Grooming powder can be used on especially soft coats that are prone to matting; it will help separate the hairs, soak up excess natural coat oils, and make combing and brushing easier. Sprinkle the powder on and work it into the coat with your fingertips before brushing and combing it all out.*

2 *Comb out loose hair without pulling on any knots, as this will be painful for the cat. Gently tease these out by holding the hair near the skin with one hand while combing with the other. Don't tug at a knot.*

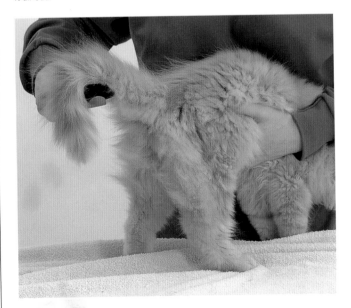

4 *Use a soft brush on the tail, too, as it is very sensitive.*

5 *Wipe around the eyes and nose with cotton balls moistened with lukewarm water (squeeze the excess out). Use a fresh cotton ball for each eye and the nose. Wipe very gently under the tail with another cotton ball, then use a dry cotton ball to dry the areas wiped.*

3 *With a soft bristle brush, gently brush the belly.*

6 *A toothbrush is ideal for grooming the facial area. Finish off by stroking the cat all over with a grooming pad to leave a smooth, shiny finish to the coat. If the claws need trimming, do this last (see page 109).*

When to groom

Once a week for shorthaired cats should be sufficient, whereas longhairs ideally should have daily attention. The more often you do it, the easier and quicker it is to keep the coat tangle-free, glossy, and looking good. You need to pick the right time to groom; waking the cat up to do it is not a good idea, and neither is grooming when he is unsettled for some reason. If your cat becomes fidgety and stressed by grooming because he was not accustomed to it from an early age, do it in short, frequent sessions to gradually get him used to the process.

Never force the cat to be groomed; wait until he's in an amenable mood before trying again. Offering tiny morsels of his favorite food can help settle him and take his mind off what you're doing as well as help him associate grooming with something rewarding and pleasurable.

It can be helpful to have someone hold the cat, talk to him, and offer treats to distract him while you concentrate on the grooming.

Grooming short coats

Simply using your hand to groom will suffice for many shorthairs; it will loosen and stroke off dead hairs, tone muscles, and be pleasurable and soothing for both you and your cat.

Alternatively, use a moderately stiff brush to brush lightly but thoroughly from head to tail to remove any loose hairs. Pay particular attention to the throat, armpits, and inner thighs. Next, use a fine-toothed comb all over from head to tail to remove parasites, flaky skin, and loose hairs. Then use cotton balls moistened with lukewarm water to wipe around the eyes, nose, and under the tail (use a clean piece for each). Finally, wipe with a grooming pad to leave the coat soft and shiny.

Top tip

Always do a small skin patch test 24 hours before bathing your cat with a wet or dry product to be sure he's not allergic to it.

When bathing your cat, take care not to get water or soap in his ears, as all cats find this very upsetting.

Bathing

Cats usually don't need bathing (in fact, most hate being wet at all), unless:

• You are preparing for a show.
• The coat is very dirty or contaminated with chemicals or oil.
• The cat needs shampooing with a fungicidal or insecticidal wash for health reasons (in which case you should wear protective plastic gloves).

Always use a specially formulated cat shampoo and coat conditioner, never products intended for use on human hair, as these may prove harmful if absorbed through the cat's skin or accidentally ingested. You will probably need an assistant while bathing your pet, even if he has been accustomed to the procedure since kittenhood. It's easiest to bathe the cat in the kitchen sink.

• Quarter-fill the sink with lukewarm water (comfortable to the elbow-touch test) and place the cat in it.
• Pour water over the body until the fur is saturated.
• Use your hands to carefully wet the cat's face.

• Massage in the shampoo, but don't get any on the face or near the eyes.
• Refill the sink with clean lukewarm water (or use a spray attachment) and rinse all the shampoo out of the coat. You will probably have to replace the water several times to be sure no soap remains.
• If using a separate conditioner, massage this into the coat and leave for the recommended time, then rinse.
• Gently dry the cat as much as you can with a thick, warm, soft towel.
• Place him in a warm room to dry off thoroughly so he doesn't get cold.
• Once dry, groom the coat into place.

Top tip

If the cat's inside ear flaps are dirty, use a piece of cotton or a cotton ball moistened with water or baby oil to gently clean off wax or dirt. Never poke anything, such as a cotton swab, into the ear, or you could damage this delicate organ.

Frequently asked question

Q My cat hates getting wet, but for shows I need to make sure his coat is spotlessly clean. Is there an alternative to wet bathing?

A Dry brush-in/brush-out shampoos are available, as are types that can simply be sprayed onto the coat and massaged in, with no rinsing necessary; both are well worth considering.

Brushing teeth

Regularly cleaning your cat's teeth will help prevent tooth and gum disease, which can lead to mouth pain and tooth loss, and bad breath. Toothbrushes specifically designed for kittens and cats are available from pet stores or veterinarians, but a soft human toothbrush with a small head will suffice. You must not use human toothpaste; cats hate the taste and the froth it creates, and it can make them sick. You should also be sure to take your cat to the vet for regular checkups, when his teeth will be examined.

Start brushing your cat's teeth when he is a kitten so he gets used to the treatment. Begin by simply dipping the brush in warm water and placing it inside your kitten's cheek for a few seconds while gently holding his mouth closed. Reassure him with soothing words and repeat with the other cheek. Do this every day, gradually extending the period the brush is held in your kitten's mouth, until he is no longer concerned about it. At this stage, begin to move the brush in a small circle, starting with the back teeth, as these are less sensitive than the front teeth. In a few weeks, you should be able to brush both the front and back teeth without upsetting the kitten. At this stage, you can introduce a small amount of feline toothpaste. Alternatives to a toothbrush include a piece of gauze wrapped around your finger or a rubber fingertip "cap."

Brushing your cat's teeth with a child's soft toothbrush (or one designed for cats) and special toothpaste formulated for felines (never use one intended for humans) helps prevent the tartar buildup on teeth that leads to tooth and gum disease. In order to be able to do this safely and effectively, ask your vet or a veterinary nurse to show you how.

Did you know...?

Giving your cat a small strip of raw meat every day to chew on will help keep his gums and teeth in good condition. Suitable meats include poultry, rabbit, or beef that has been deboned.

Travel

There are going to be occasions when you need to be away from home, such as vacations, visiting friends and family, going into the hospital, or business trips, and you will have to make arrangements for your cat to be looked after. There are several options to choose from (see the checklist), depending on the circumstances.

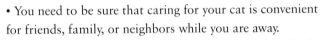

Checklist

✓ boarding facilities
✓ friends, family, or neighbors
✓ pet-sitters
✓ taking the cat with you

Thinking ahead

Whichever option you choose, make the arrangements well in advance because:

• You will need to be sure your pet's vaccinations are up to date.
• You may need to get a pet passport if taking your cat overseas.
• Good boarding facilities get booked up quickly for peak times, as do pet-sitters, and you need to check them out first.

• You need to be sure that caring for your cat is convenient for friends, family, or neighbors while you are away.
• If you intend to take the cat with you, you need to check whether your accommodations are suitable for cats.
• You need to get your pet used to traveling.

Boarding facilities

Seek recommendations for local boarding places from vets and cat-owning friends, neighbors, and relatives, then visit them first to check them out for yourself. Your cat will need to be vaccinated against relevant diseases beforehand, so be sure his inoculations are up to date well in advance. Take

Feline fact

An older cat may be a problem at vacation times, as he may not do well in a boarding facility. If this is the case, having someone come in daily to keep an eye on him and provide for his needs may be the best option if you are going to be away for more than a couple of days. This will avoid any major disruption to your cat's life, but it's not the same as having company at home and may work only if your pet is used to letting himself in and out of the house through a cat flap. An indoor-only cat may be lonely and become depressed in this situation, so a pet-sitter may be a better choice.

Taking the cat's bed, bedding, and favorite toys along to a boarding facility will help him adjust and feel more at home.

Did you know...?

If your cat has a contagious disease, such as feline leukemia (see page 173), boarding facilities won't accept him for fear of him passing the condition on to others. In such circumstances, you will have to make alternative arrangements when you are away. Similarly, if your cat is ill when you deliver him, the proprietor has the right to refuse to take him.

the vaccination certificate when you take your pet to the facility, as they will want to check that it is current.

Look for a boarding facility that provides individual quarters and an outside run for each cat. The indoor space should be clean, warm, and dry, with room for a bed, litter box, food and water bowls, and toys. The run should be secure and large enough for the cat to get some exercise, with a scratching post and a ledge or other area on which he can sun himself and take in the view. Facilities with only indoor quarters aren't ideal, since inadequate airflow may increase the possibility of infection spreading among the cats.

Pet-sitters

A good option, particularly if you have a number of pets, is to arrange for a pet-sitter to stay in your house if you're going to be away for any length of time. Although this can be expensive, it does give you peace of mind knowing that both your pet and your house will be well looked after. Be sure to use a reputable agency—ideally one recommended

by word of mouth—that chooses its staff carefully and offers insurance in case of any mishaps.

Pet-sitters are trained to look after all sorts of animals, with some specializing in and preferring particular species, so ask for someone who is cat-oriented. You can find pet-sitters advertised in cat magazines and on the Internet.

Having a reliable person come in at least twice a day to feed and water, clean out litter boxes, and provide affection can be an ideal solution for cats who don't do well away from home.

Top tips

If you are leaving your cat in the care of someone while you are away, give them the following details before you depart:

• feeding and litter-box cleaning routine

• any specific dos and don'ts regarding your pet's care

• medication information, if your cat is receiving any

• contact details for you in case of an emergency

• contact details for your vet (provide a map of how to get there if the person isn't familiar with the area)

• your cat's insurance details, if applicable

Cats should always be transported in a secure carrier. The more used they are to traveling, the less disturbing they will find it.

Taking the cat with you

If you want to take your cat away with you on a regular basis within your own country, you need to get him used to traveling, whether by car or public transportation. Train him to accept this from an early age by taking him out for short trips. Check with public transportation companies regarding pet travel, as some have specific rules and regulations about this.

To help the cat feel secure, put his blanket and favorite toy(s) in the carrier. Be sure the car is not too warm and that there is plenty of ventilation so the cat doesn't become heat-distressed. Never let him out of the carrier except in an emergency. Taking a folding pen with you can be a good idea so the cat is secure in your hotel room when you are not there.

Taking a cat overseas

Recent changes in legislation now allow for pet travel without the need for quarantine in many countries. Find out what the regulations are in your country, since the rules regarding pet travel vary and are constantly being updated and reviewed. To do so, contact the relevant government department (in the United States, it's the U.S. Department of Agriculture Animal and Plant Health Inspection Service). The Pet Travel Scheme (PETS) now applies to pet cats and dogs who live in a PETS-qualifying country. Before you attempt to take your cat out of your country and bring him back in again, you must find out:

• what, if any, restrictions apply

• what you need to do to comply with rules regarding pet identification, vaccination, and parasite treatment

• how far in advance you need to take care of medical requirements

Frequently asked question

Q   I would like to take my cat away with me on weekends. Is this a good idea?

A   Bear in mind that being territorial creatures, some cats don't adapt very well to being removed from their home ground; they can become very upset, which will lead to a miserable time away from home for all concerned. Outgoing, confident cats who are very owner/people-oriented tend to be better at coping with travel than more shy and retiring ones. If you understand your cat well, you will know whether taking him with you would be a good idea or not. Some hotels and other types of accommodation welcome pets and have facilities to care for them.

AT-A-GLANCE VACATION CHECKS

CARE OPTIONS	PROS	CONS
Boarding	• Least hassle to arrange • Safe and secure • You know cat will be looked after properly • Should he become ill or injured, he will receive appropriate, immediate treatment	• Expensive • Cat must be vaccinated • Disease-carrying and ill cats will not be admitted • Risk of contracting disease • Cat may pine
Hiring a pet-sitter	• Cat will have experienced company and care all the time • No need to vaccinate • Your house will also be looked after	• Expensive • You may not want a stranger in your home
Having a visiting caretaker at home	• No cost • Cat can remain in familiar surroundings • No need for vaccinations, if you are against them	• Cat will not be supervised all the time • An only cat may get lonely • Can you rely on the caretaker to see to your cat at least once a day and care for him properly? • If cat becomes ill or is injured, he may not get immediate, appropriate treatment
Having your cat stay with a caretaker	• No cost • Cat will possibly have company all the time • No need to vaccinate	• Cat may escape and get lost • Cat may not adjust well in unfamiliar territory and become depressed or develop behavior problems
Taking your cat with you	• You know cat is receiving proper and appropriate attention • Cat will have company all the time	• It can be difficult to find cat-friendly accommodations • Organizing PETS eligibility when going overseas (see page 118) can prove expensive and complicated • Cat may escape and get lost • He may not enjoy traveling • He may not adjust well • He may contract a disease

HEALTH CARE

Like every other mammal, the cat has a skeleton that protects his internal organs; this enables him to live and reproduce. Powerful muscles are attached to the skeleton to allow motion. The cat mates with the opposite sex, and the female bears live young, which are suckled and reared by the mother until they are able to survive alone.

All cats, whatever their breed, share the same physiology (the way in which a living creature functions); they differ only in minor ways to produce a more compact or elongated conformation, with some displaying differences in fur, balance, or bone structure caused by particular mutations or selective breeding.

Many medical problems can be avoided by ensuring that a cat has a good diet and adequate exercise and by being aware of early symptoms that all is not well.

From routine parasite control to vaccination, reproduction to neutering, this section of *Essential Cat* tells you all you need to know about feline physiology and health.

The feline body

The feline body is a remarkable feat of natural engineering that has evolved into an animal possessing great beauty, grace, and athletic prowess. To keep your cat in peak condition, it helps to know how his body is constructed and how it works, how to recognize when something is wrong, and what to do when he is ill or injured. Whatever the species, members of the *Felidae* family are characterized by the elements in the checklist.

Checklist

- ✓ a slender yet strong and supple body
- ✓ a short, round head in proportion to size
- ✓ erect ears that are broad at the base and taper upward
- ✓ powerful legs, especially the hind legs
- ✓ dense fur
- ✓ whiskers
- ✓ great climbing and leaping agility
- ✓ five toes on the front paws and four on the rear
- ✓ sharp, curved claws that retract (except in the cheetah) on all toes
- ✓ 16 teeth in the upper jaw, 14 in the lower

Bones

A cat's body may be much smaller than a human's, but it contains more bones—some 230 to a human's 206. The skeleton of a cat is made up of a semi-rigid framework that supports other, softer structures.

The bones of the spine, limbs, shoulders, and pelvis (working together with muscles and tendons) comprise a system of efficient levers to aid movement, while the skull, ribcage, and pelvis protect the major organs they contain.

There are four distinct types of bones—long, short, irregular, and flat—and each type has a particular function. They are joined together by tendons and ligaments to make up the skeleton.

Bones in the feline body

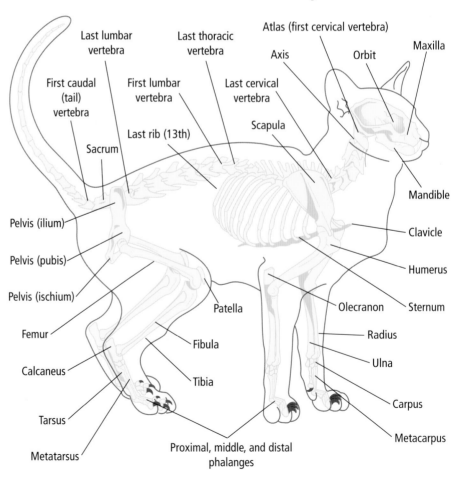

Long bones

These are cylindrical and have hollow shafts that contain the vital bone marrow in which blood cells are manufactured. They form the cat's limbs. Feline long bones are the humerus, radius, femur (thigh bone), tibia, and fibula.

Short bones

These consist of a spongy core surrounded by compact bones. They are the bones in the feet and the patella (kneecap, where the femur joins the tibia).

Irregular bones

So called because of their irregular shapes, these bones are similar in structure to short bones. A long string of irregular bones forms the spine (vertebral column) and tail. The irregular projections of the bones in the spinal column serve as attachment points for the various muscles of the cat's back.

Flat bones

These are made of two layers of compact bone with a spongy layer sandwiched between them; they comprise the skull, pelvis, and shoulder blades (scapulae). Flattened and elongated bones make up the cat's 13 pairs of ribs; these bones are not hollow but contain a substantial amount of marrow, which produces blood cells.

Ligaments and tendons

Ligaments are short bands of tough, fibrous tissue that connect bones or cartilage or hold together a joint. They are also membranous folds that support organs and keep them in position.

Tendons are flexible but inelastic cords of strong fibrous tissue that attach muscles to bone.

Muscular system

Overlying the skeletal framework is a complex network of muscles that gives the cat his powerful and graceful movement and is responsible for his sinuous shape. There are three types of muscle in the feline body: cardiac, smooth (involuntary), and striped (voluntary).

Cardiac muscle

This specialized muscle forms the heart and possesses unique powers of rhythmic contraction to pump blood around the body through a network of arteries and veins. A cat's heart works in the same way as a human heart, with four chambers and a double pump.

When jumping down, a cat stretches his body down as far as possible before pushing off, to reduce the distance covered and the shock of landing. Powerfully muscled hind legs allow the cat to leap up to five times his own height. Cats' finely tuned sense of balance enables them to land precisely where they want to.

Smooth (unstriated) muscles

These carry out muscular functions not under the cat's control and include the muscles of the intestines and walls of blood vessels. They are also called involuntary muscles.

Striped (striated) muscles

These are muscle tissues in which the contractile fibers are arranged in parallel bundles (hence the term "striped") and are attached to the limbs and other parts of the anatomy that are under the voluntary control of the cat. They are also known as voluntary muscles.

Voluntary muscles are usually attached to bones that form a joint. Extensor muscles extend and straighten a limb, while flexor muscles flex and bend the joint. Muscles that move a limb away from the body are called abductors, and adductors move it back in again. There are more than 500 voluntary muscles within a cat's body, enabling him to be fluid in his movements.

Respiratory system

Respiration provides the cat's body

Powerful muscles at the root of the tail, combined with small muscles and tendons along the length of it, enable the cat to move his tail expressively and use it as an important balancing aid.

with the oxygen that is vital for life. During respiration, the cat draws in air through his nose and mouth. This air passes through the throat (pharynx) and down the windpipe (trachea), through the bronchi and into the lungs. In the lungs, gaseous exchange takes place: carbon dioxide from the blood filters into the air sacs as oxygen passes from the air to replenish the blood. The used air is then exhaled. Breathing is automatic: Chest muscles contract and relax, acting like a pump on the ribs and diaphragm and driving air in and out of the lungs. The breathing rate varies in each individual and depends upon:

• age
• exercise
• emotion
• environmental temperature

The normal respiration rate of a healthy, resting adult cat is 20 to 30 breaths per minute.

Frequently asked question

Q Why are cats' bodies so flexible?

A Compared with most animals, cats have small collarbones and more supporting muscle. Their shoulders, therefore, are not rigid; this gives them great flexibility when grooming or twisting and pouncing on toys and prey. Special vertebrae in the spine allow cats to twist and flex much more than they would be able to with a more rigid backbone.

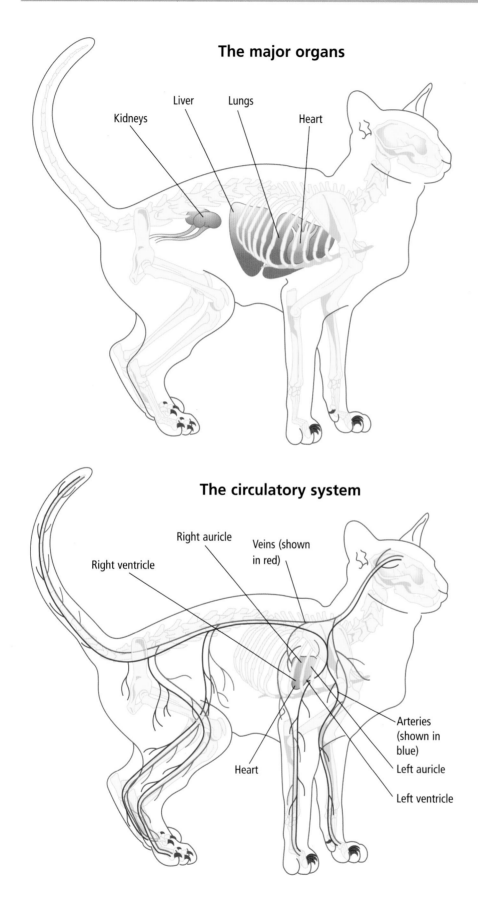

The major organs

Kidneys
Liver
Lungs
Heart

The circulatory system

Right auricle
Veins (shown in red)
Right ventricle
Arteries (shown in blue)
Left auricle
Heart
Left ventricle

Circulatory system

Every body cell needs nourishment, and this is supplied by the blood, which delivers it and also removes waste products from the body. Blood is made up of red blood cells and white blood cells that are contained in a fluid called plasma. Plasma contains platelets, which contain a blood-clotting agent for use in the event of cuts and wounds.

Red blood cells transport oxygen, while white blood cells collect and transport impurities and bacteria that have invaded the red cells.

Incredible journey

Blood is continually pumped around the body via the four-chambered heart, its journey beginning in the left auricle (upper chamber). Enriched with oxygen from the lungs, the blood from the left auricle travels into the left ventricle (lower chamber) and on into a great artery—the aorta. It runs its course quickly through all the arteries and arterioles and into a fine network of capillaries throughout the body, distributing its store of oxygen and nutrients as it goes. As it releases these, the blood collects waste matter (bacteria, dead blood cells, and carbon dioxide).

Leaving the capillaries, the blood enters tiny veins (venules) where it begins to slow down, laden with waste products, before passing into the great veins that transport it back to the lungs to dump its rubbish and be replenished with oxygen and nutrients. From here it enters the heart to repeat its journey.

Why cats are usually sleepy after meals

Extra nutrient-rich blood is required by different parts of the body at different times. After a heavy meal, for example, the cat's abdomen draws in extra blood to aid digestion, at the expense of the supply to the brain and other parts of the body. Hence the need of the cat (and other animals) to rest or sleep after eating: The brain is less active, and energy is being utilized for digestion rather than for other activities.

Pulse

Blood passing through the aorta causes its walls to expand, and a pressure wave (pulse) passes down the arteries. In a healthy adult cat at rest, the pulse rate is 160 to 240 beats per minute, depending on environmental temperature and the cat's emotional state at the time.

Digestive system

The cat's digestive system is adapted for a meat-eating hunter who may not always be successful in catching a meal and may occasionally gorge at a large kill. His mouth construction means that a cat tears or bites at his food, then swallows it quickly, giving the salivary juices virtually no time for the preliminary breakdown of starches into blood sugars. Any starches present in the cat's diet are therefore of little nutritional value.

Feline gastric juices are more powerful than those of a human; they are, in fact, strong enough to soften bone. Cats can swallow large chunks of prey creatures (rodents and birds), and any parts—such as feathers, hair, and bones—that are not quickly broken down in the stomach may be regurgitated.

In the stomach, protein is broken down into simple amino acids (basic constituents of proteins). These are then combined to form the building blocks necessary for replacement of cells throughout the cat's body. From the stomach, partly digested food passes through a valve called the pylorus to the small intestine. Further digestion takes place, aided by secretions from the pancreas and liver. Fats are broken down and extracted, sugars are changed structurally (ready for storage), and minerals are absorbed.

From the small intestine, the now-fluid food contents pass into the large intestine, where they are acted upon by the specialized bacteria present there. Excess water is drawn off and utilized where appropriate, and the waste passes through the colon to be voided as feces (solids) or as urine (liquid).

Feline fact

Cats can swallow and digest their food without chewing it.

Teeth

Feline teeth are designed to stab, slice and tear at raw, tough, and "chewy" food rather than chew it, and these actions help keep the teeth in good condition. Kittens shed their baby (milk) teeth as their permanent ones come through at around six months. When kittens are born, the teeth are just visible inside the gums, and soon erupt. At six weeks old, a kitten's teeth are strong and needle-sharp, so for obvious reasons, a mother cat will become reluctant to feed her babies, and a natural weaning process takes place, ideally with the youngsters having strips of raw meat to chew on.

Occasionally, "double dentition" occurs, when a kitten does not shed

The skull and teeth

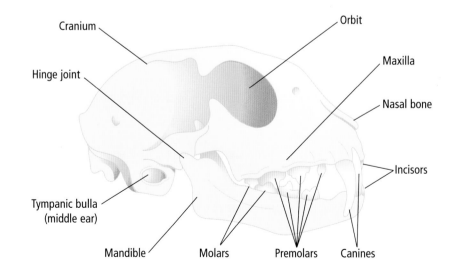

Cranium

Hinge joint

Tympanic bulla (middle ear)

Mandible

Molars

Premolars

Canines

Incisors

Nasal bone

Maxilla

Orbit

his milk teeth. It may be necessary for a vet to remove the milk teeth so they don't interfere with secondary tooth growth and action, which could ultimately lead to digestive and other health problems.

Paws and claws

A cat's forepaws are made up of sets of three small bones, each of which forms a digit corresponding to the finger of the human hand. The tiny bones at the end of each digit are highly specialized and articulate so that the claws may be extended or retracted at will. The cat has no thumb, but a corresponding digit comprises two bones to form the dew claw. In the hind feet, the bones are longer and the first toe is absent altogether.

Claws are made up of keratin (the same material that forms hair) and grow continuously from the base, like human fingernails. There are five claws on the forepaws but only four on each hind paw; the fifth claw acts rather like our thumb, helping cats to grip when they climb and hold prey.

Extra digits (polydactyly)

Occasionally, a cat has more digits than is normal on either or both of the front and rear paws. This anomaly sometimes occurs in crossbreds and is nothing to be concerned about (being no more than a gene mutation) because it usually doesn't affect a cat's health or movement. If, however, this condition occurs in pedigreed cats, it has more serious implications for the breeder, though not for the cat. The cat will not conform to breed standards and will have little value. Pedigreed cats who are afflicted should therefore not be bred, so they don't perpetuate the condition.

Skin and fur

Feline skin is made up of two layers of tissue: the dermis (inner layer), and the epidermis (outer layer), which is constantly being replaced as it dies and sloughs away as tiny flakes of dandruff (dead skin). There are sweat glands on the skin, but these seem to exist mainly for excreting impurities from the body rather than for controlling body temperature. True sweat glands are found in the foot pads.

Sebaceous glands open into the hair follicles and produce a semi-liquid, oily substance called sebum, to coat each new hair as it grows. Scent glands can be found on the

Did you know...?

The hairless skin (known as leather) of the cat's nose and paws is extremely sensitive to the touch.

The skin and fur

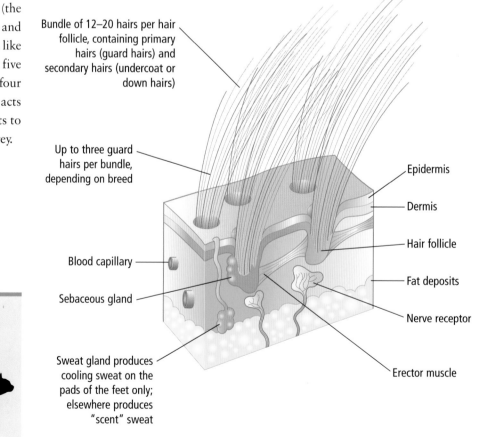

Bundle of 12–20 hairs per hair follicle, containing primary hairs (guard hairs) and secondary hairs (undercoat or down hairs)

Up to three guard hairs per bundle, depending on breed

Blood capillary

Sebaceous gland

Sweat gland produces cooling sweat on the pads of the feet only; elsewhere produces "scent" sweat

Epidermis

Dermis

Hair follicle

Fat deposits

Nerve receptor

Erector muscle

forehead just above the eyes (temporal glands), by the lips (perioral glands), and near the root of the tail.

Hair is derived from the outer layer of skin and acts as insulation. It is modified in certain areas to provide eyelashes, eyebrows, and whiskers. There are three main types of hair.

• **Down hairs**, or undercoat hairs, are the shortest, thinnest, and softest hairs; they lie close to the body and conserve body heat.
• **Awn hairs** form the middle coat and are slightly more bristly, with a swelling toward the tip before tapering off. They are partly for insulation and partly for protection.
• **Guard hairs** are the thickest, longest, and straightest; they form the top coat, which protects the fur below from the elements.

The ratio of down, awn, and guard hairs varies greatly among domestic breeds; in the wildcat, there are approximately 1,000 down hairs to 300 awn hairs and 20 guard hairs. Muscles attached to the large follicles

enable the hairs to become erect and stand out at right angles to the skin; this occurs, for example, when the cat is alarmed or ill and has an abnormal temperature.

All hairs, especially the guard hairs, are sensitive to the touch, but even more sensitive are the **vibrissae** (whiskers, eyebrows, and similar hairs on the cheeks, chin, and behind the

Whiskers on the sides of the face determine whether a space is wide enough for the cat to get through; if the head and shoulders fit, the rest of the body will be able to follow.

forelegs), which are bigger and thicker. Whiskers are deeply embedded in the upper lip and are surrounded by a mass of tiny nerve endings that transmit information about any contact they make and changes in air pressure around them. The vibrissae also act as guides when it's too dark to see, enabling the cat to move without banging into objects.

Cats shed dead hair constantly, especially if they live in centrally heated environments, but those who spend a good deal of time outdoors will grow a thicker winter coat and then shed this as the temperature warms up again in spring. It's not unusual for their coats to look quite patchy during this time.

Top tip

In a fit, healthy animal, the skin is pliable; in a sick or dehydrated cat, it's stiff and unyielding. A sudden change from the normal pale pink color can indicate illness and needs veterinary investigation.
• **White** can indicate anemia due to parasite infestation, dietary deficiency or shock.
• **Reddening** indicates inflammatory disease of the skin or underlying tissues.
• **Blue** indicates heart trouble, respiratory disease, or poisoning.
• **Yellow** indicates jaundice (liver dysfunction).
Any change of color in the cat's skin is usually first noticed on the ear flaps, nose, lips, and gums.

Feline senses

The nervous and sensory systems of the cat are essential to his health and well-being. Perceptions and reactions to his environment are dependent on his senses, movement is controlled by the central nervous system (brain and spinal cord), and the endocrine system (hormone-producing glands) controls his behavior patterns. The five faculties by which a cat's body perceives his surroundings are on the checklist.

Checklist
✓ sight
✓ smell
✓ hearing
✓ taste
✓ touch

The central nervous system

This controls and coordinates the cat's everyday activities. Information received by the sensory organs is constantly monitored by the nervous system and dealt with according to its importance: it's acted upon immediately, discarded, or stored away for future use, as appropriate. The brain has three clearly defined regions: the fore-brain, the mid-brain and the hind-brain.

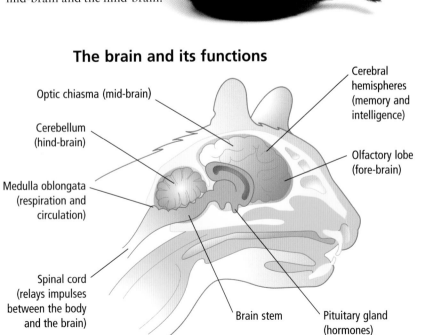

When familiar cats meet, sniffing each other confirms visual recognition and gathers information about how the other cat is, where he has been, and what he has been doing.

The brain and its functions

Optic chiasma (mid-brain)

Cerebellum (hind-brain)

Medulla oblongata (respiration and circulation)

Spinal cord (relays impulses between the body and the brain)

Brain stem

Pituitary gland (hormones)

Cerebral hemispheres (memory and intelligence)

Olfactory lobe (fore-brain)

Feline fact

The pads of a cat's feet are very sensitive and have many touch receptors. Some cats behave strangely just before an earthquake hits; perhaps they can detect vibrations of the earth through their sensitive foot pads.

The central nervous system

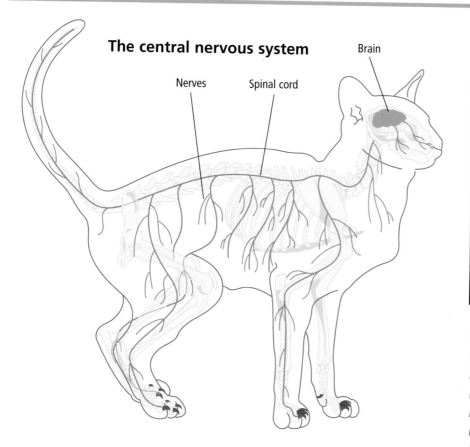

Nerves   Spinal cord   Brain

The pupil of the eye opens very wide to admit more light, which passes through the transparent cornea and lens to the retina at the back of the eye. Any light not absorbed by the retina bounces back to a layer of cells known as the tapetum lucidum, which reflects it back to the retinal cells, reinforcing the information transmitted to the brain by the nerves there. Any reflecting light still not absorbed creates the effect of the cat's eyes shining yellow, green, or red at night.

Fore-brain

This area is concerned with the sense of smell via the olfactory lobe, as well as memory and intelligence. It also contains the thalamus (which responds to impulses traveling from the spinal cord) and the hypothalamus (which controls the internal regulatory processes).

Mid-brain

This area contains the optic lobes and deals with signals stimulated by light, so it's responsible for sight.

Hind-brain (core)

Here, the cerebellum controls balance, and the enlarged end of the spinal cord forms the medulla, controlling the respiratory and circulatory systems. The pituitary gland (which produces hormones) is situated in this region, as is the limbic system that controls digestion.

Unsurprisingly, this part of the brain is vital for the survival of the cat.

Sight

Cats need only one-sixth of the light humans need in order to distinguish the same details of shape and movement. The eyes face forward, allowing fields of vision to overlap and giving stereoscopic vision that is slightly wider than ours. This enables the cat to be accurate in judging distances for jumping or springing and pouncing when hunting.

Being comparatively large and set in deep skull sockets, feline eyes do

Frequently asked question

Q Why does my cat lie in very hot places, like in front of the fire, without appearing to feel discomfort?

A The ancestors of our domestic cats were originally desert-living animals. Consequently, they are comfortable lying in front of an open fire, close to a radiator, or even on a surface that is heated to a temperature too high for humans to stand.

The eye

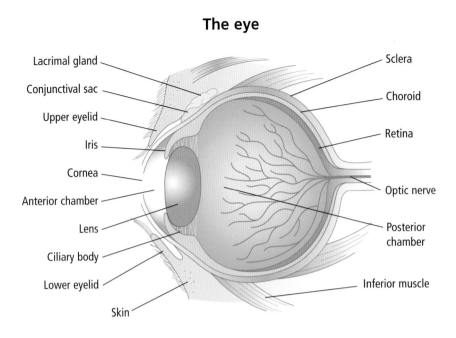

Lacrimal gland
Conjunctival sac
Upper eyelid
Iris
Cornea
Anterior chamber
Lens
Ciliary body
Lower eyelid
Skin

Sclera
Choroid
Retina
Optic nerve
Posterior chamber
Inferior muscle

Feline fact

When a cat is out of condition or ill, a tiny pad of fat beneath the eyeball contracts and causes it to retract slightly into the socket, which results in the haw extending partially across the eye. Being able to see the haw, therefore, is taken to be an indication of ill health.

not move freely, so the cat turns his head to bring objects into sharp focus. Cats are not color-blind, but they see the world in more subtle shades of color than we do. Their eyes are protected from strong light by the iris contracting to form a slit-like pupil, limiting the amount of light reaching the delicate mechanisms at the back of the eye; when the iris contracts, the sharpness of vision is enhanced. In addition to the upper and lower eyelids, there is a third eyelid, which is called the nictitating membrane, or haw. This is a thin sheet of pale tissue tucked away in the corner of the eye. Its function is to remove dust and dirt from the cornea by moving across the surface of the eyeball during any inward movement and to keep the eye moist and lubricated.

Smell

The feline sense of smell is about 30 times more developed than that of humans, and it's essential to cats in relation to their sex life and hunting for food and water. A thick, spongy membrane (olfactory mucosa) in the nose, with over twice the surface area of that in humans, contains 200 million scent-sensitive cells. When minute particles of odorous substances in the atmosphere are drawn in during normal breathing, they stimulate highly sensitive nerve endings of fine hairs within the nasal cavities.

In the roof of the mouth, there is a special organ lined with receptor cells. Known as the Jacobson's organ, it is a tube ½ inch (1.2 centimeters) long,

A cat's positive response to fresh meat is more likely to be evoked by smell than by taste.

Did you know...?

• Cats rarely eat carrion and find the smell of tainted or medicated food highly offensive. Thus, they will rarely eat food that isn't fresh or has been treated with a worming product or other medication.

• The area in the nose for detecting scent is ten times larger in cats than it is in humans. They also have a correspondingly larger part of the brain to help them decipher scent messages.

with its opening just behind the front teeth. Interesting odors are sucked into the mouth and directed to the Jacobson's organ to be investigated in more detail. The facial expression cats adopt to do this (mouth open, lips drawn back, and nose wrinkled) is called the Flehmen reaction.

Hearing

Feline hearing is exceptionally well developed, and cats can hear noises that are quite inaudible to the human ear. They can hear ultrasonic sounds that precede an activity, which is why they often react before we are even aware that anything is happening. The ear is made up of three sections: the outer, middle, and inner ear.

The outer ear

The ear flap (pinna) acts as a funnel to direct sound waves down to the eardrum, which is tautly stretched across the ear canal, separating it from the middle ear. The eardrum vibrates in response to sound waves.

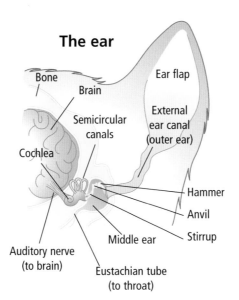

The ear

Bone
Brain
Semicircular canals
Cochlea
Ear flap
External ear canal (outer ear)
Hammer
Anvil
Middle ear
Stirrup
Auditory nerve (to brain)
Eustachian tube (to throat)

The middle ear

Here, three small bones—the hammer (malleus), anvil (incus) and stirrup (stapes)—transmit the sound relayed from the eardrum to the cochlea, which is within the inner ear.

The inner ear

The cochlea is a spiral cavity containing the organ of Corti, which converts the sound vibrations transmitted from the middle ear into nerve impulses. These are then passed along the acoustic nerve to the auditory cortex of the brain, where they are decoded and recognized by comparison with sounds stored in the memory bank.

Taste

It seems that the cat's tongue can differentiate among food items that taste salty, sour, bitter, or sweet. Most cats appear to like salty things, but

Large ear flaps help a cat focus sound and judge where it is coming from, thereby enabling him to pinpoint the position of prey even if he can't see it.

they can vary considerably in their reaction to sweet foods. Taste alone does not seem to be important to most cats, but this is how tiny kittens, on first leaving the nest, test most new surfaces and objects—by licking them carefully, methodically, and with great concentration. Just how the information received in this way is analyzed and stored is not known, and it occurs only during the most sensitive period of learning in the young cat.

Touch

Cats use their noses, paws, and whiskers to examine objects by touch, after having first checked them out by smell. They rarely burn themselves with hot foods or liquids, since they use their noses as thermometers to test for temperature. Affectionate cats will often pat at their owner's faces or bodies to attract attention. Hunting cats touch prey with a paw to see if it is dead or alive. Mother cats often touch their kittens with their faces and paws. Cats also use their faces, whiskers, and paws to touch each other.

Top tip

It is cruel to trim a cat's whiskers. Although the actual process of trimming them would not hurt, the cat would be left without vital sensors on his head to judge space on either side of him and how close he is to objects in the dark.

Routine health care

Knowing your cat and his usual behavior will help you recognize when something is not quite right with him. If ailments are spotted quickly, early treatment often helps to prevent more serious problems, which usually results in less suffering for your pet and smaller veterinary bills for you. Monitoring your cat's mood and habits and carrying out simple health checks on a regular basis will enable you to assess his state of health. Things to look out for are shown in the checklist.

Checklist

✓ general condition, skin, and coat
✓ appetite and thirst
✓ grooming
✓ mouth and teeth
✓ eyes, ears, and nose
✓ weight
✓ feces and urine
✓ ease of movement

Regular home checks

Keep an eye on all the following aspects of your cat's health, condition and demeanor.

General condition, skin, and coat

A healthy cat is alert, interested in what's going on around him, and curious, and he looks well. The skin should be clean, supple, and pliable, while the fur should be soft and glossy, not dull and lank. Check thoroughly for parasites, wounds, flaky skin, lumps, and scabs (see also "Top tip" on page 129).

Appetite and thirst

Any change from normal eating and drinking patterns can indicate a digestive, urinary, or mouth problem, so if you notice this, it's essential to take your cat to a vet as soon as possible.

Grooming

A healthy cat constantly cleans and grooms his coat. A sick cat neglects himself in this department and soon begins to look scruffy. Reasons for failure to wash include mouth soreness and joint stiffness (which could indicate arthritis), while female cats who stop cleaning their genital area could have a distasteful discharge.

Mouth and teeth

Cat breath should not be offensive: tooth and gum problems are easy to diagnose because of the resulting

Cats who are ill or in pain often withdraw into themselves and become quieter and depressed. If your pet has lost interest in life, seek veterinary advice. Checking your pet's vital signs (see page 99) on a regular basis can help alert you to early signs of problems.

If your vet knows your cat almost as well as you do, this familiarity often makes treating him more efficient and successful.

Top tip

If, for any reason, you feel that you would like a second veterinary opinion, you are entitled to ask for one, and your vet can arrange it. No one vet knows everything there is to know about his particular field of work. Your vet may even suggest consulting another expert in order to treat your cat most appropriately, especially if your vet doesn't have the specialized equipment or knowledge to deal with your cat's specific health problem.

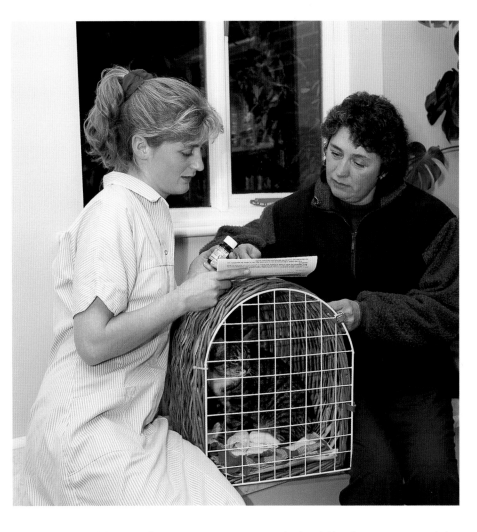

unpleasant smell. The gums and tongue should be pale pink. White gums indicate anemia; red, bleeding gums are an indication of gingivitis (see pages 164–65); and blue or gray gums suggest a circulatory problem. If your cat shows a reluctance or inability to eat, seek veterinary advice, as this could be due to a mouth abscess, a broken tooth, or a more serious ailment.

Eyes, ears, and nose

The eyes should be clear, bright, and free of discharge. Some breeds of cat with "typey" facial features often have eye discharge as a result of the skull structure being deformed in such a way that tears can't drain away

as they would normally. Tear stains can be removed with cotton dipped in clean, boiled and cooled water. Any clouding of the surface of the eye requires veterinary attention. The

pupils should be the same size and the third eyelid (haw) retracted.

The inner ear surface should be clean, smooth, and odor-free and feel slightly greasy to the touch. Smelly

Frequently asked question

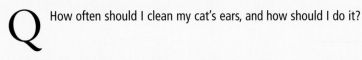

Q How often should I clean my cat's ears, and how should I do it?

A Cats don't usually need help cleaning their ears. However, if the inside of his ear flaps (pinnas) look dirty, you can gently clean them with a cotton ball moistened with baby oil. Never poke cotton swabs or anything else into the ear, or you may damage it. If you have any concerns about the cleanliness of your cat's ears, consult your vet.

Raised haws (third eyelids) are an indication of ill health.

Did you know...?

A cat who has been to the vet for any reason may come back smelling very different and may be treated like a stranger by other cats in the household. Separating them and transferring their scents to each other with a clean cloth can help reintegrate them.

Administering medicine and pills

Give medication only as prescribed or advised by your vet, and administer it as directed. It helps to have someone hold the cat while you medicate him.

Using a syringe (your vet can supply these) is the easiest way to administer liquid medicine. Insert the nozzle in the corner of the mouth and squeeze a little at a time, stroking the cat's throat to encourage him to swallow.

Administer pills using a pill-syringe (obtainable from vets) or with your fingers, although the latter can be more difficult. Tip the cat's head back as shown and insert the pill on the back of the tongue, then gently hold the mouth shut.

To encourage the cat to swallow the pill, gently stroke his throat.

or dirty ears need veterinary investigation, as this suggests there may be infection.

The nose should be clean, slightly damp, and free of discharge. Runny noses are often a sign of viral infection or allergy.

Weight

Cats, like humans, vary greatly in size and conformation. The average adult weight of a cat is 9 to 11 pounds (4 to 5 kilograms); a small cat may weigh only 5½ pounds (2½ kilograms) and a large one as much as 12 pounds (5½ kilograms). Your vet will be able to tell you what your cat's ideal weight should be, and any deviation from this should be closely monitored. Obese cats have a shorter life expectancy than those of the correct weight, as carrying excess

Applying topical treatments

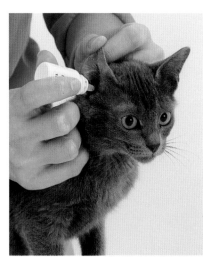

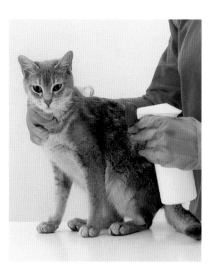

Use only treatments prescribed by your vet and apply them as directed.

When administering drops or ointment to the eye, hold the cat's head still and aim for the center of the eye.

To apply ear drops, hold the head still, squeeze in the drops, and gently massage the base of the ear to be sure the liquid is evenly distributed in the affected area.

Wear rubber or plastic gloves to protect yourself when applying flea spray, massage it into the coat, and wash your hands thoroughly afterward.

weight puts strain on the heart and limbs. Weight loss can indicate internal disease, a parasite, or a pancreatic problem.

Feces and urine

If your cat has difficulty defecating or urinating, he needs urgent veterinary attention. Stools should be firm, not hard or loose, while urine should be pale yellow and free of clouding and an offensive smell. Both should be free of traces of blood.

Ease of movement

Stiffness when moving around may indicate joint problems. Limping suggests a direct pain source such as a fractured limb, a wound, a thorn stuck in the foot pad, or an infected claw bed. A general reluctance to

move, combined with crying out when picked up or even when touched, may be due to an internal injury or ailment.

Veterinary health checks

Choose a vet who specializes in feline health and make the effort to cultivate a good relationship. Owners

Symptoms of concern at a glance

- Bad breath or bleeding gums
- Blood in urine or feces
- Breathing difficulty
- Coughing or sneezing
- Diarrhea or constipation
- Difficulty eating
- Difficulty eliminating
- Dullness or fever
- Fur loss or failure to groom
- Haws visible
- Increased or decreased thirst

- Lameness
- Loss of appetite
- Marked change in behavior
- Nasal or eye discharge
- Pallor of lips and gums
- Excessive scratching or licking
- Signs of acute pain
- Stiff or unsteady gait
- Swollen abdomen
- Vomiting
- Weight loss or gain

who take their cats for regular health checks and routine vaccinations and seek advice on parasite control and dental care are valued customers to whom a vet will be prepared to give more time.

Take your pet for a checkup at least once a year (combine this with the annual vaccination booster), or every six months for cats age 10 or more; this can often identify health problems before they become serious. Keeping a diary of your pet's behavior and health and being able to explain any changes you have noticed and when they first occurred is very useful in helping your vet treat your cat appropriately and swiftly when the need arises.

Parasite control

Cats, especially those with outdoor access, can be plagued by a variety of external and internal parasites, including lice, fungal infections, fleas, ticks, and worms—all of which cause ill health. Pet stores and supermarkets carry a wide variety of preparations to treat parasites, but most are not as effective as those that are available by prescription from your vet. So, while the former may be cheaper and easier to obtain, they often turn out to be false economy in the long run.

Never use more than one flea treatment at a time, or your cat may overdose. You must also treat the indoor environment where your cat lives, or reinfestation will occur immediately. Vacuum carpets and wherever your cat likes to sleep regularly, and wash your pet's bedding once a week or so to destroy flea eggs.

Intestinal worms (roundworms and tapeworms) are most efficiently controlled with all-in-one treatments prescribed and administered by your vet. A typical worming regimen is to treat kittens aged 4 to 16 weeks for roundworms every 2 weeks; from 6 months old, treat the cat every 2 to 6 months (depending on whether he is an outdoor or indoor cat) for both roundworms and tapeworms. Consult your vet for advice about the most appropriate worming plan and treatment for your cat.

Vaccination

Cats, like other animals, are susceptible to certain viral diseases, some of which can prove fatal. While they can't pass these on to humans (apart from rabies), they can transfer them to other cats, either in the air or through mating or other physical contact. It is advisable to have your cat vaccinated, when possible, in order to:

• help prevent your cat from dying early from a feline viral disease
• help keep feline viral diseases from reaching epidemic proportions

Feline fact

There have been numerous cases where owners of both cats and dogs have tried to save money by treating their cats with flea treatments formulated for dogs—and ended up with dead cats. Never treat your cat with anything other than preparations formulated for felines.

• help eliminate feline viral diseases
• enable you to board your cat when you go on vacation
• enable you to enter cat shows
• enable you to travel overseas with your cat if you desire

When to vaccinate

Vaccinations are given by injection by a vet. Kittens can receive their first shots at about 9 weeks of age, with a second dose given at 12 weeks. Full protection is not achieved until 7 to 10 days after the second vaccination. Thereafter, cats should receive

Diseases your cat can be vaccinated against

• Feline leukemia virus (FeLV); see page 173.
• Cat flu (feline respiratory disease). There are two forms of this disease: feline herpesvirus (also known as feline rhinotracheitis virus) and feline calicivirus (FCV); see page 164.
• Feline distemper, also known as feline enteritis or feline panleukopenia; see page 171.
• Chlamydial disease; see page 169.
• Rabies.
• Feline infectious peritonitis (FIP). A vaccine is currently available only in the United States; see page 173.

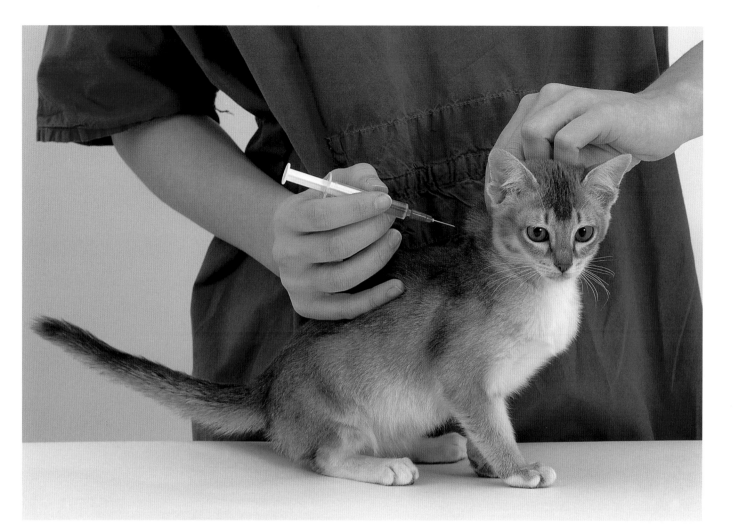

Ideally, cats should be 100 percent well before vaccinations are given, to reduce the risk of an adverse reaction.

annual or biannual (depending on the vet and whether tests are carried out to ascertain the level of immunity) both to maintain their immunity and satisfy boarding facility, passport, and show-entry requirements.

Vet clinics, rescue groups, and pet stores in many areas offer low-cost vaccinations; ask your vet for infomation or look for signs or flyers in local stores.

Vaccination risks

There are some risks associated with vaccination, but these are generally low, and severe reactions are rare. The cat may have a small lump at the injection site or may be quiet and off his food for 24 hours after immunization, but he should soon recover. If you're worried about your pet's behavior or health after vaccination, contact your vet immediately for advice. On the whole, most vets recommend immunization to prevent certain feline diseases from reaching epidemic proportions, especially in urban areas where there are large numbers of cats.

Did you know...?

Some insurance companies will not pay for treatment if a cat is not vaccinated, so check all of the policy clauses before parting with your premium. Shop around to find the best policy at the right price. Vets may be able to advise you on the most efficient insurance companies to use, since they deal with them frequently.

Neutering

If you are going to breed your cat, you have a clear idea of whether you want to raise kittens or set up a stud. If not, and your cat is to be only a pet, he or she should be neutered in order to help prevent the situations in the checklist.

Checklist

✓ unwanted kittens
✓ potential behavior problems, such as spraying in the house
✓ spread of disease
✓ straying
✓ the characteristic pungent male cat smell
✓ health risks during pregnancy and birth
✓ females continually calling for a mate when in season

Why neutering is a good idea

A fully mature, unneutered male cat spends a good deal of his time trying to pass on his genes. To do this well, he needs to defend a sizable territory, compete with rivals, and court females. Since all of these require large amounts of energy, tomcats often look thin and ragged, with numerous scars and abscesses from countless fights. Straying, too, can become a real problem with both male and female cats as they seek mates (see page 86).

As well as the risk of unwanted kittens, there is also the real risk of cats, particularly feral cats, passing on diseases against which there is no vaccination and for which there is no cure. One such disease is caused by the feline immunodeficiency virus (FIV)—the feline equivalent of humans AIDS (although there is no danger of humans contracting FIV from a cat).

Neutering your female cat removes the great responsibility of having to find good, loving homes for kittens.

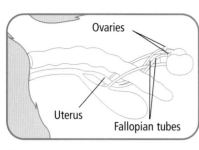

Queen

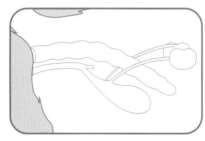

Spayed female

Spaying

Before spaying: The female reproductive tract comprises the ovaries, fallopian tubes, and uterus (womb).

After spaying: The ovaries, fallopian tubes, and uterus have been removed.

Castration

Before castration: The male reproductive tract comprises two testicles (testes) within a skin sac (scrotum), connected to the penis via the vas deferens (spermatic cord).

After castration: The testicles and part of the vas deferens have been removed.

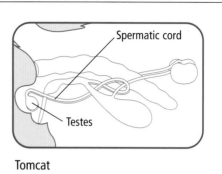

Tomcat

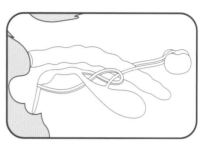

Neutered male

When to neuter

Neutering (known as spaying in females and castration in males) should be done when the cat reaches sexual maturity at about six months (the equivalent of adolescence in humans) or at any time afterward. Individual vets have their own policies on spaying in-season females; because the reproductive organs are engorged with blood at that time, surgery may be more risky. The neutering of pedigreed or show cats is often delayed to allow their full physical development.

What's involved?

Because the operation is more invasive for female cats, spaying is more expensive than castration. Some animal groups sponsor low-cost neutering programs to help owners who otherwise couldn't afford the surgery. Ask about this at your local animal clinic or contact animal groups in your area.

Spaying females

The vet removes the ovaries, fallopian tubes, and uterus under a general anesthetic. After the operation site is shaved and cleaned to help prevent infection, he makes a small incision on the midline (from the navel toward the hind legs) in order to remove the relevant organs. The wound is closed with two or three stitches, which are removed about a week later; with soluble suture material, which gradually dissolves on its own; or with surgical glue.

Castrating males

The vet anesthetizes the cat and removes his testes and part of the spermatic cord through an incision in the scrotum; this incision is so small that it doesn't even require stitches.

Did you know...?

A female keeps coming into season (also called heat) every 3 weeks during the breeding season (early spring to late autumn) unless she becomes pregnant. When she is in season, she makes a distinctive loud call to alert toms in the vicinity that she's looking for a mate.

As they stray to find mates, unneutered cats run a greater risk of contracting diseases from other felines as well as being involved in fights or being injured or killed by cars.

Pre- and postoperative care

The cat must go without food and water for 12 hours before surgery, but most cats are up and about, eating, drinking, and playing, within a few hours of the operation. Females who have had a midline incision may take slightly longer to recover—about 48 hours.

When you bring the cat home from the vet's, he or she will probably still be drowsy from the anesthetic, so provide a warm, quiet place to rest undisturbed—with water, a litter box, and a light meal of cooked white fish or chicken—until your cat feels ready to join the family again. Your vet will advise you whether you can let the cat outside. Gently discourage the cat from nibbling or excessively licking any stitches. If you have any concerns following neutering, be sure to contact your vet for advice.

Behavior

If neutered as kittens, male and female cats will behave almost the same as before, at least from the practical point of view of an owner. Minor changes to expact are:

• Their territories are much smaller than those of unneutered cats.
• Territorial fights may still occur but will be much less of a problem.
• Both sexes tend to be more affectionate and amenable.
• They tend to spend more time at home.
• Although neuters may spray urine if they are emotionally disturbed by something, their spray smells nothing like the strong urine of an unneutered male cat, which is also sticky and difficult to clean from household furnishings.

There is some truth in the observation that neutered cats become more inactive than unneutered ones as they age,

Feline fact

If you have a female in season, known as "heat" or oestrus, visiting toms will loiter around her territory, and you will have to put up with their spraying. There may be fights in the vicinity, as well as loud, persistent caterwauling during the night. Female cats sometimes also develop the habit of spraying when their hormonal balance has been upset either by doses of contraceptive medication or by frequent periods of season.

although their life expectancy is greater. You may have to adjust a neutered cat's diet, as well as encourage daily play and exercise.

Contraception

It is possible to administer a hormone treatment to female cats to prevent unwanted pregnancies, but there are drawbacks to prolonged birth-control treatment. It could cause fertility problems if you wish to breed the cat later; it could also result in side effects that include increased appetite, weight gain, lethargy, behavior problems, and uterine disease.

It's also possible to use contraceptive drugs to prevent an unwanted pregnancy once mating has taken place (misalliance)—rather like the human "morning-after" pill. This involves the vet giving an injection of hormones that override the queen's own hormones, making her body

Top tip

Pedigreed stud cats are kept confined to prevent them from contracting infection from other cats and getting into fights. Although they have never experienced freedom, many of their natural desires will be frustrated, so it's kinder to castrate them once their breeding days are over.

believe she has not become pregnant. This causes her to come into season again. Vets don't like to give this treatment, since it can have serious side effects, such as the development of pyometra (a life-threatening infection of the uterus).

Frequently asked question

Q I have heard that it's best for a female cat to have a litter before she is neutered. Is this true?

A This myth is based on human needs rather than scientific fact, as there is no evidence to suggest that it's necessary. If you want to raise a litter and are confident that you can then place the kittens in good homes, spay the female soon after weaning to prevent any further pregnancies.

A cat born in early spring may come into season during the following autumn, whereas one born later in the year may not do so until the following spring. Some cats, depending on the breed, may come into season earlier than normal, at 5 months, while others may not do so until they are as old as 12 months.

REPRODUCTION

Once the female is ready, matings are repeated 10 to 20 times a day for up to six days. Only fit, strong males can sustain this, which means that kittens in the same litter can sometimes have several fathers. This promiscuous behavior ensures not only that the chances of conception are maximized but also that the kittens have a variety of physical and personality traits to increase the next generation's chances of successful procreation.

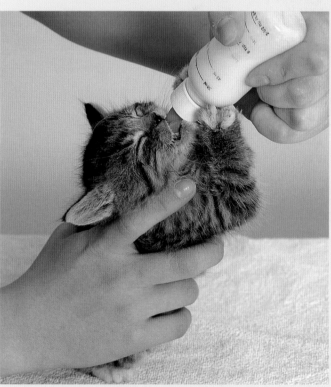

Mating and conception

As the female (queen) becomes ready to mate, she rolls flirtatiously on the ground to attract males. (Queens should be wormed well before mating takes place.)

Cat courtships can be prolonged affairs: despite wanting to mate, the female does not immediately accept the male's approach.

When she does accept him, the male firmly grips the back of her neck to hold her steady as he mounts her and mates.

As the male withdraws after mating, barbs on the end of his penis (which stimulate the female to ovulate) cause pain inside the female, making her cry out and turn on him in self-defense. At this point, the male makes a hasty exit in case the female strikes out at him, and his involvement in the reproduction process is complete.

After copulation, the female rolls on the ground and then washes herself. Minutes later, she may be ready to mate again, thus increasing her chances of successfully becoming pregnant.

Pregnancy and birth

The gestation period in cats is nine weeks (approximately 65 days). Movement of the fetuses can be felt from the seventh week of pregnancy. As the birth nears, the female will begin to "nest" and seek a private, preferably dark, safe place in which to give birth.

Once first-stage labor starts, the queen paces around, crying or growling softly and looking behind her in an agitated and puzzled manner. As second-stage labor begins, the queen goes into her nesting area or box, lies on her side, and strains as uterine contractions move the kittens, one at a time, down the birth canal.

After delivering a kitten, the queen cleans away the birth membranes covering him, thus allowing and stimulating him to breathe. She passes the placenta, joined to the kitten by the umbilical cord, and eats it, severing the cord close to the kitten's body.

Once the kittens are born, the queen cleans herself, then settles down to suckle her babies, curling herself around them, and rests for about 12 hours.

Pregnancy, birth, and kitten care

The urge to reproduce and pass genes on to the next generation is strong in unneutered cats, and a healthy female with access to males and a plentiful food supply can produce two or three litters a year. Species survival depends upon procreation, and pregnancy and birth are the most natural things in the world. Left to their own devices, cats engage in noisy courtship, with several males trying to mate with an in-season and responsive female, but usually one male is able to keep the others away and mate successfully.

Caring for the pregnant queen

Apart from increasing her diet (see page 42) with food specially formulated for expectant queens to cope with the demands being made on her body, treat the mother as usual during pregnancy. About halfway through the pregnancy, she will become more careful about jumping and passing through narrow openings, in deference to her enlarged shape.

Be very careful when picking her up and cuddling her as her pregnancy progresses; she may not appreciate either, being uncomfortably full of kittens. If she becomes constipated, replace one of her daily meals with oily food, such as sardines, to help relieve the problem.

Prepare a nesting box and place it in a quiet and undisturbed area of the house. A large, sturdy cardboard box will do, with a hole cut into one side 6 inches (15 centimeters) off the ground and wide enough for the cat to pass through easily. Line the base with newspaper for insulation and place a thick layer of paper towels on top to make a soft, absorbent, and disposable mattress for the

1 day old
A newborn kitten can't see and has very little control over body movements.

10 days old
His eyes usually open about now.

3 weeks old
The kitten starts to experiment with solid food at this age.

5 weeks old
By now he is able to run and balance well.

8 weeks old
The kitten has learned how to socialize with his siblings and other pets in the household.

birth. Show the queen where the nest is, but bear in mind that she may ultimately choose her own place—which could even be on or under your bed.

With longhaired queens, clip the hair surrounding the birth canal (to aid hygiene and ease of delivery) and nipples (to facilitate suckling). Gently sponge her anal area twice a day if she is carrying a large litter and is unable to clean herself. Make sure she is free of fleas and mites in the 10 days preceding birth; consult your vet regarding suitable treatment.

Did you know...?

Some queens may develop mastitis due to a bacterial infection. Symptoms include hard, hot teats that produce bloodstained or abnormal-looking milk. The affected cat will seem out of sorts and may vomit and have little or no appetite. Veterinary attention should be sought immediately so the queen can be appropriately treated and the vet can show you how to hand-strip her teats and hand-feed the kittens if necessary.

14 weeks old
The kitten's motor skills have improved, and his ability to balance is at its peak.

5 months old
He may reach sexual maturity at this age, though it varies from cat to cat.

1 year old
The cat is now an adult, with full size and maturity.

Newborn kittens' eyes are sealed shut and begin to open at about 10 days old, although it may happen as early as the middle of the first week. A kitten can't see with clarity or accuracy until he is about 4 weeks old; at 15 days old, his ears are open and fully functional. Milk teeth begin to appear when the kittens are about 14 days old. Young kittens should be wormed, with veterinary advice, while still nursing, if necessary.

Labor and birth

Females give birth and raise their young following instinctive behavior patterns that allow them to do so unaided, although they do get better with practice. In a natural colony of cats, however, other related females will help out, acting as midwives and surrogate nurses while the mother takes a break. This cooperation ensures greater protection and survival of the young.

Labor and birth normally proceed easily. Once second-stage labor begins (when the queen goes into the nesting box and lies down), a whole litter may be born in an hour or so, or they may be spread over 24 hours with long rests between kittens.

Birth problems

Occasionally, things do go wrong. If the queen has been straining hard for two hours without results, call the vet immediately. Sometimes, for various reasons, kittens do not survive. If the bereaved mother cat appears distressed, contact your vet for advice; the queen may require medication to suppress her milk and help prevent mastitis, or the loss may have a happy ending if the vet knows of orphaned kittens needing a foster mother. Other problems that can arise during pregnancy or following birth include:

Did you know...?

False pregnancies can occur in cats. Also known as pseudo or phantom pregnancy, this condition is quite natural and may occur in a queen who has failed to conceive during a season. In some cases, the owner may not notice any difference in the female's mental or physical state; in other queens, the false pregnancy can result in a swollen abdomen and mammary glands that fill with milk. In the latter case, the cat may also spend time nest-building and crying and be reluctant to exercise; she may even display the pushing actions of an actual birth. Such queens often form attachments to inanimate objects, such as toys, and some have invisible "kittens." In severe cases, veterinary advice and treatment where necessary should be sought.

Until the kittens are old enough to relieve themselves outside of the nest, the mother licks them after each feeding to stimulate them to eliminate, swallowing the wastes to keep the nest hygienic.

Queens move their kittens if they do not feel safe or if the nest becomes dirty or flea-infested. The kittens go limp when she picks them up by the scruff of the neck, which does not hurt them and helps her carry them more easily.

Feline fact

Once mating has taken place, the male cat plays no further role except to defend the territory where his females raise their young from other marauding males, who may kill the kittens so that they can perpetuate their own genes.

• **Miscarriage** due to illness or because the fetuses are not healthy.

• **Uterine infection** after birth, indicated by fever, vomiting, lack of appetite, and dark vaginal discharge.

• **Prolapsed uterus**, indicated by a swollen red mass appearing out of the vulva.

Consult your vet immediately if any of these occur.

Mother and baby care

Kittens are totally dependent on their mother and her milk for the first three weeks. After this, they begin to experiment with eating the solid food that their mother brings back, in the form of prey, or that their human caregiver provides. The mother will eat and drink more than normal to maintain a plentiful milk supply. Four good meals daily should be enough for her, depending on the number of

Frequently asked question

Q A friend's cat died of eclampsia and she had to raise the kittens herself. What is this condition, and what should I do if my pregnant queen gets it?

A Also known as milk fever or lactation tetany, eclampsia is caused by a severe calcium deficiency. It can occur up to 21 days after kittening, or occasionally, just prior to kittening. Seek veterinary attention immediately.

Symptoms of eclampsia include salivation, anxiety, aversion to light, lack of co-ordination, high temperature, and convulsions. If the condition is not quickly treated with calcium and glucose injections, the queen will die.

Orphaned kittens

In the rare instances when unweaned kittens are abandoned or orphaned, it's necessary to hand-raise them. This is hugely time-consuming and tiring, although usually it's ultimately rewarding if the helpless babies grow into healthy and independent young cats. If kittens are left without a mother for whatever reason, consult your vet immediately. She may know of a potential feline foster mother, be able to put you in touch with an experienced breeder for tips, or offer advice on how to hand-raise the kittens.

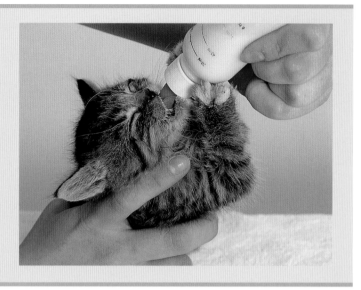

When you are hand-raising, kittens need feedings every two hours for the first week.

kittens. Give her small meals of fresh food, preferably one formulated for lactating queens, to make sure she receives the nutrients she needs to maintain her own body as well as her offspring.

Keeping kittens clean is a vital role for the mother, whose kittens may otherwise die of disease. She continues to wash them all over until the babies learn how to clean themselves.

Early learning

Begin to handle the kittens from two weeks old to start the vital feline-human socialization process. At this age, the mother cat will not be too anxious about familiar humans touching her babies. By the age of three weeks, kittens can stand quite well and toddle around on short, unsteady legs. At this stage, they can roll over and right themselves and play with their siblings with paw pats and bites. By the fourth week, the kittens can move around confidently, and they can often run and balance well by the end of the fifth week. However, it will be another five to six weeks before they can run, jump, and leap with accuracy, balance, and coordination.

Weaning

At four weeks, the kittens start to explore outside the nest and to experiment more with solid food (see pages 40–45 for feeding guidance). Supply them with food specially formulated for kittens to make sure they receive the nutrients their rapidly growing bodies need.

As they eat increasing amounts of solids, their excretions change and their mother stops cleaning up after them, so provide them with their own litter box. If they don't learn to use it from their mother, place them on it after every meal; leaving a small amount of waste in the box from their last elimination will help them recognize where to go at first.

Queens naturally wean their kittens themselves as their milk gradually dries up five to six weeks after the birth. At this age, the kittens should be fully weaned to solid kitten food, although they may still return to Mom for the occasional comfort suckle if she allows it. By eight weeks, the kittens are usually fully independent of their mother for food and hygiene and are ready for new homes. (For information about kitten care from eight weeks onward, see pages 102–9.)

Top tip

When playing with her babies and teaching them to fight, the mother can sometimes appear to be quite rough, even making them squeal, but she's not really hurting them, so this is nothing to be alarmed about.

A large cat pen, complete with litter box, in which to put the kittens for brief periods when weaning begins will provide the mother cat with periods of much-needed rest; it will also encourage the kittens to use the box.

Did you know...?

If kittens are unwanted, and you can't place them with a new owner or a shelter, veterinary euthanasia is the legal and most humane method of disposing of them. Consult your vet or local animal shelter.

The mother encourages her kittens to play from an early age—as soon as they start to toddle around. Through play, the kittens practice social, fighting, and hunting skills to equip them for adult life.

FIRST AID AND ILLNESS

Despite your best efforts, things can often go wrong, and it's wise to be ready for any eventuality concerning the health of your cat. Try to minimize the possibility of accidents occurring around your home, and be vigilant about checking for any signs of ill health that may need attention.

First aid

A knowledge of first aid can prove useful and, in some instances, essential. Accidents tend to happen when we least expect them to, so it's sensible to be prepared. Emergency situations need immediate action; if you know what to do, you may be able to limit the injuries sustained by your pet and perhaps even save his life. The checklist shows the basic steps to take when administering first aid.

Checklist

- ✓ always remember that your own safety is paramount
- ✓ assess the situation
- ✓ protect yourself and others from injury
- ✓ examine the cat
- ✓ diagnose injuries
- ✓ treat injuries or pain as appropriate
- ✓ keep the cat warm, calm, and quiet
- ✓ protect the cat from further injury
- ✓ contact a vet for professional advice and treatment

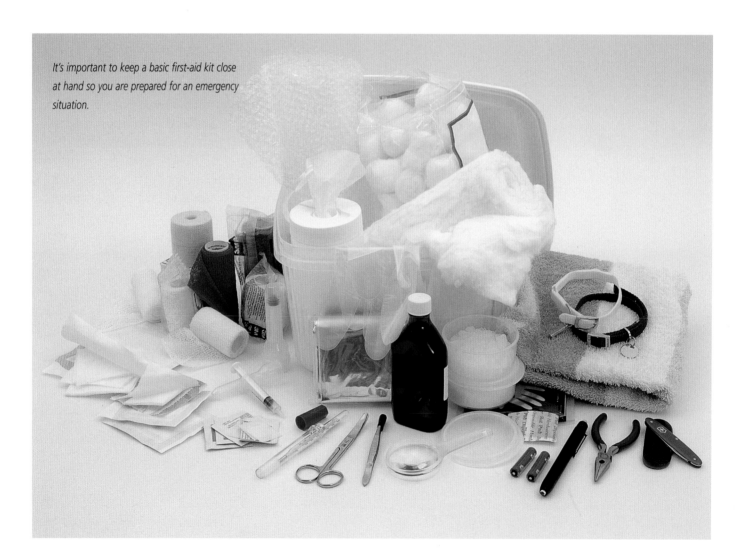

It's important to keep a basic first-aid kit close at hand so you are prepared for an emergency situation.

First-aid training

Having basic training in the subject will give you the confidence to deal with an emergency situation calmly and efficiently until an expert practitioner can take over from you. Some vet clinics run courses in basic first aid, and it's well worth enrolling in one of these. Practicing first-aid procedures on a healthy cat when you're not under pressure is the best way to learn what to do in a real situation.

First-aid kit

It is useful to have a home first-aid kit with which you can treat minor injuries and minimize adverse effects on the cat. Basic first-aid items can be bought from your vet, local drugstores, or good pet stores. A first-aid kit should contain the following:

- **Absorbent paper towels** to wipe up any liquid mess
- **Alcohol** to remove ticks
- **Antihistamine** to ease insect stings and bites
- **Antiseptic lotion** for cleaning wounds, particularly animal bites
- **Antiseptic wound powder** for treating wounds and promoting healing
- **Bandages** to keep dressings in place
- **Blunt-tipped tweezers** to remove ticks or insect stingers
- **Cat claw clippers**, preferably the guillotine type
- **Conforming (self-adhering gauze) bandage** to hold dressings in place
- **Cotton balls** to bathe eyes, clean wounds, and use as a dressing (dampen first to prevent strands from breaking off and sticking to a wound)
- **Cotton swabs** to remove grass seeds or other foreign objects from the eyes (dampen first)and to clean wounds and apply ointments
- **Curved, blunt-tipped scissors** to clip fur and trim dressings to size
- **Elizabethan collar** to prevent a cat from interfering with dressings or sutures
- **Glucose powder** to make a rehydrating fluid (mix 1 tablespoon of glucose with 1 teaspoon of salt in 1¾ pints/1 liter of warm water)
- **Heavy-duty protective gloves** for restraining a cat
- **Nonstick dressings** for bandaging cuts
- **Pen-light and batteries** to inspect the mouth and ears

An Elizabethan collar stops a cat from scratching his head or chewing stitches. You can buy them from your vet or a pet store or make one from a plastic bucket by slitting it down one side and cutting a hole in the center to fit around your cat's neck; alternatively, use a piece of strong cardboard.

- **Petroleum jelly** to lubricate thermometer before insertion
- **Small stainless steel or plastic bowls** to hold saline or antiseptic solutions when bathing wounds
- **"Space blanket" or large sheet of plastic bubble wrap** to maintain body temperature in cases of shock and hypothermia
- **Squares of clean cotton material** to place over wounds or stem blood flow (old cotton or flannel bed sheets are ideal)

Did you know...?

To clip fur around wounds, use a pair of scissors with curved blades and blunt tips. Dip the blades in clean, preferably boiled and cooled water, then carefully clip the fur around the wound; the fur will stick to the wet blades, preventing it from falling into the wound. Dip the scissors in the water again to rinse off the clippings.

- **Sterile eye wash**, such as contact-lens saline solution
- **Sticky surgical tape** to hold dressings in place
- **Surgical gloves** to use when treating wounds
- **Syringe or eye dropper** to administer liquid medicine
- **Table salt** to make saline solution (2 teaspoons of salt dissolved in 1¾ pints/1 liter of warm water) with which to clean wounds and counter infection
- **Thermometer** to check temperature (rectal types are cheaper, but aural, or ear, types are easier to use)
- **Towel** to wrap the cat in when administering medication and to restrain him in the event of accident

First-aid basics—ABC

The basics of first aid for a cat are as simple as ABC—airway, breathing, and circulation. The first priority is to make sure that the cat's airway is clear so he is able to breathe, and that he is breathing. Next check that his blood is circulating properly (his heart is beating). You can then

deal with any other symptoms as appropriate.

Airway and breathing

If the cat is unconscious, check that he is breathing. If there is little or no breathing and the tongue is blue-black, open the mouth and remove anything that may be blocking the airway. Gently lift the chin to extend the cat's neck to open the airway. If he still does not breathe, administer **artificial respiration**:

1 Hold the cat's mouth shut and cover his nose with your mouth.
2 Gently breathe up the cat's nose—30 breaths every minute (taking your mouth away from his nose between breaths to allow him to exhale).
3 Continue until the cat begins to breathe on his own, veterinary help arrives, or you believe the cat to be beyond help.

Circulation

Next, check for a heartbeat. Put your ear on the cat's chest on the left side, just behind his elbow, and listen. Also check for a pulse: Place a couple of fingers in the same place as you put your ear or on the inside of the cat's thigh in the groin area (see page 99). If there is no heartbeat, begin **chest compression**:

1 Place one hand either side of the cat's chest, just behind his elbows.
2 Squeeze the chest smoothly, giving two compressions every second (always use the flat of your hand—never the fingers). Don't use too much force, as it is easy to break the ribs.

Top tip

One way of checking whether a cat is breathing is to place a small mirror close to his mouth and nose; if it mists and clears, he is breathing.

Cover an unconscious cat with a blanket, towel, or even a sweater to keep him warm while awaiting veterinary attention.

A sick cat is seldom cooperative. He feels vulnerable and defensive, so beware of his claws and teeth when handling him or doing something he doesn't feel happy with. Always wrap him in a towel for your own protection.

Top tip

A seriously injured or dangerously ill cat is better nursed at an animal hospital than at home, where full facilities and veterinary skills are not available.

3 Give two breaths for every four compressions. Keep this up until the cat's heart begins to beat, you can't do any more, or a vet takes over. Keep checking for a heartbeat or pulse throughout your attempts at heart massage.

Moving an injured cat

Approach the injured cat carefully, looking for any signs of injury and assessing any danger to both yourself and the cat. Speak softly and reassuringly to help soothe him and keep him calm.

If the cat is in the street, move him to the side if it's safe to do so. Try not to aggravate any injuries when picking him up; the best way to do this is to slide a board under him as a makeshift stretcher or slide both hands under him, keeping him in a horizontal position. A common injury when a cat is hit by a car is a ruptured diaphragm, so it's very important to keep the cat horizontal to keep his internal organs immobile.

Emergency situations

Advice on what to do in a number of first-aid situations is given below.

Car accidents

As well as checking for obvious signs of injury, inspect the back of the neck for lumps and swelling that may indicate broken bones or trauma. Seek veterinary attention as soon as possible, informing the vet of any signs or symptoms of injury you have spotted. Even if the cat appears to have no external injury, a thorough veterinary checkup is essential in case there is unseen internal hemorrhaging, which could be life-threatening if not detected and treated as soon as possible.

Burns and scalds

Cool the burned area with ice water (if you can stand the cat in a tub or sink, pour this on for about 10 minutes) to reduce the pain and the severity of the burn. Cover the burn lightly with a cool, damp, clean cloth (handkerchief or dish towel), wrap

the cat in a space blanket (or equivalent), place him in a warm carrier, and take him to the vet without delay.

Chemical burns

Put rubber gloves on and wash the affected area under cold running water, either by standing the cat in the tub or sink and running water over the burn or by using a hose in the yard. Prevent the cat from licking the area and follow the instructions for burns and scalds.

Sunburn

Treat as for burns and scalds.

Poisoning

If you suspect your cat has ingested a poisonous substance (profuse salivating is the most obvious sign; extreme sleepiness is another and is commonly associated with rat poison), contact your vet immediately, giving the name of any poisons you suspect. This will allow the vet to obtain any relevant information from the poison

A cat with broken bones will not be easy to handle and may bite and scratch anyone who tries to approach or move him.

manufacturer or poison control center while you transport your cat to the office. If you are instructed by the vet to make your cat vomit in order to rid his digestive system of as much of the poison as possible, place one or two small washing soda (sodium carbonate) crystals, if you have them, at the back of his throat. Alternatively, use mustard or salt mixed with a little water. Get the cat to the veterinary clinic without delay. Keep all hazardous substances securely locked up, especially when there are curious kittens in the house.

Broken bones

Signs of fractured bones—apart from them protruding from the skin—include extreme pain on moving a limb, swelling, tenderness, loss of control of and/or deformity of the limb, unnatural movement of the limb, or the sound of the two ends of the bone grinding against each other (called crepitus). Keep the cat as quiet and warm as possible and take him to a vet immediately.

Electrocution

Once the power supply has been turned off, check that the cat is breathing; if not, begin artificial respiration (see page 158). If it's not possible to switch off the power supply, do not approach the cat. Electrocution will almost inevitably cause burns, which will need treatment as detailed on page 159. A big danger in treating cats who have been electrocuted is the threat to the first-aider. It's easy to rush in to help the stricken animal without considering any risk to yourself—so think before you act.

Insect stings and bites

A cat will frantically claw at the area of his body where he has been stung. If he has been stung in the throat, seek immediate veterinary attention, since swelling may block the airway and kill the cat. For stings elsewhere on the body, clip the fur from around the affected area so you can see what the problem is, then wash it with saline solution. Bees leave their stingers in the victim but wasps do not. If you can see the stinger and judge it is removable with tweezers, then do so carefully and wipe the area with cotton dampened with alcohol.

To neutralize the effect of a wasp sting, wipe the area with vinegar or lemon juice; use bicarbonate of soda dissolved in a little water for bee stings. Then dry the area thoroughly but gently and apply a wet compress to help reduce the irritation and swelling. For other insect bites, clean and dry the area, then apply antihistamine spray or ointment to reduce itching and irritation.

Animal bites

Cats are at risk from bites by other cats and by rats. If you suspect your cat has been bitten by another cat, clip the fur from around the bite and clean the wound thoroughly with saline solution, followed by diluted antiseptic lotion. Dry the area, then apply a liberal dusting of antiseptic wound powder. Repeat twice daily—it's important to keep the wound clean, or it may become infected and result in an abscess. Cat bites almost always end up infected if they are not treated adequately.

Rat bites are especially dangerous, since these rodents carry many harmful diseases. Treat immediately as for cat bites, then take your pet to a vet, who may administer an antibiotic injection and prescribe an antibiotic dusting powder for the wound.

In areas where venomous snakes live, it's not unusual for cats to attack them and be bitten in the process.

Snake bites

It's extremely important to keep the injured cat as calm as possible and prevent him from running around or even making any movements in order to limit the circulation of the venom through his body. Try to remain as calm as possible and seek immediate veterinary attention.

Drowning

Pull the cat out of the water and hold him upside down (if possible) to drain the water from his lungs. Then lay him flat and rub his body fairly vigorously to promote respiration. If he isn't breathing, start artificial respiration (see page 158) and get veterinary help as soon as possible.

Foreign bodies

In most cases, it's best to leave the removal of foreign bodies lodged in the cat's body to a vet—contact your veterinary clinic for advice. If the cat is pawing at the affected area, gently restrain him to prevent further damage until your vet takes over and deals with the problem. You can sometimes flush grass seeds out of the eye, using a syringe filled with saline solution, and extract thorns from paws fairly easily, but check that the end has not broken off and been left in the wound. If this happens, seek veterinary treatment, or it may fester.

Choking

Choking warrants immediate action: Taking the cat to a vet will waste time and may result in death from asphyxiation. Securely wrap the cat in thick material and open his mouth to see if there is anything stuck in his throat. The main worry is that in trying to remove a foreign object, you will push it farther down the throat and make matters worse. If you have a helper, have him hold the cat's mouth open while you remove the blockage.

If whatever is blocking the airway is wedged in place, do not try to pull it, or you may cause more damage. Instead, with the cat on the floor in front of you but facing away from you, sit down, lift the cat's hind legs, and hold them between your knees. Place one hand on either side of the chest and squeeze, using jerky movements, to try to make the cat cough. Squeeze four or five times, and the cat should cough out the object. Let your cat rest, then take him for a

Frequently asked question

Q How loose or tight should bandages be?

A If you haven't had a veterinary first-aid course, bandaging is best left to vets and veterinary nurses, since incorrect application can do more harm than good by restricting blood circulation. Ask your vet clinic to show you what different bandages are used for and how to apply them correctly.

veterinary checkup. If the object doesn't come out, take the cat to the vet immediately.

Lameness

Check for foreign objects lodged in a limb or paw and for broken bones. Seek veterinary attention as soon as possible.

Fits and convulsions

Limit how far the cat can move by putting him in a large, well-padded cardboard box. Seek veterinary attention immediately. Seizures are extremely serious and potentially life-threatening.

Shock

Shock following an accident, injury, or terrifying experience causes an acute drop in blood pressure and is life-threatening. Signs of shock include cool skin; pale lips and gums (due to a lack of blood circulation); faint, rapid pulse; and staring but unseeing eyes. Keep the cat quiet and warm by wrapping him in a space blanket (or equivalent), and promote blood circulation by gently but firmly massaging his body, taking care not to aggravate any injuries. Seek veterinary attention as soon as possible.

Bleeding wounds

Most cuts and lacerations heal on their own fairly quickly; treatment consists simply of keeping them clean with cotton dampened with saline solution. Initial bleeding, which may be profuse, helps clean the wound of debris, thus lessening the possibility of infection. Seek veterinary attention immediately, however, if:
• The wound is spouting bright red (arterial) blood in jets.

Clean any wounds carefully with saline solution and cotton.

• There is a constant flow of dark red (venous) blood that refuses to stop.
• The wound is deep or serious enough to cause concern; sutures may be required.
• Gunshot wounds are suspected.
• The skin has been punctured. These wounds appear tiny on the surface but can be quite deep and are thus particularly prone to becoming infected. Never attempt to remove a foreign object from such a wound, since this may aggravate the injury and/or allow heavy bleeding to occur (while it is in place, the object acts as a plug and may prevent massive blood loss).
• Cuts affect toes or a limb; tendon damage may have occurred.

In the case of minor wounds, you can stem the blood flow using gentle direct pressure with a dampened clean pad of cotton material before cleaning them. Where arterial or venous bleeding is present, apply indirect pressure (not on the wound itself) to the appropriate artery or vein if you can feel it under the skin on the heart side of the wound; otherwise, press a cotton pad over the wound. Elevating the injury, if possible, will enable gravity to help reduce blood flow.

Internal injuries

Signs of internal damage incude abnormal swelling of the abdomen; bleeding from the mouth, nose, ears, eyes, sex organs (not to be confused with a queen's natural estrus) or anus; bloodstained urine and/or feces; shock; or bruising on the skin. Seek veterinary attention immediately.

DON'T MAKE IT WORSE!

SITUATION	WHAT NOT TO DO
Burns	DON'T apply too much cold water at once to the affected area, since too sudden a drop in temperature may cause more disastrous problems. See page 159.
Chemical burns	DON'T attempt to treat the cat without first putting on gloves and protective clothing to prevent the chemicals from burning you.
Choking	DON'T attempt to remove an object wedged in the mouth or throat, other than by the coughing method described on pages 161–62. If this fails, leave it to a vet.
Electrocution	DON'T touch the cat without first switching off the power supply to prevent you from also being electrocuted.
Eye injuries	DON'T apply a bandage or compress if you suspect there may be a foreign body in the eye.
Fights	DON'T try to break up a cat fight using your hands; use a long broom handle or stick to separate the cats.
Fits and convulsions	DON'T attempt to restrain a convulsing cat.
Fractures	DON'T try to splint a broken bone; leave this to a vet.
Ingested string	DON'T try to pull foreign bodies from the mouth or anus if you meet with resistance; seek veterinary attention instead.
No heartbeat	DON'T attempt chest compression if you suspect a chest injury.
Poisoning	DON'T make the cat vomit unless the vet gives specific instructions.
Severe bleeding	DON'T apply a tourniquet, since it can cut off the blood flow completely, causing severe—often life-threatening—danger to the cat.
Wounds	DON'T apply direct pressure to a wound with an object embedded in it or bone protruding from it or attempt to remove any objects from wounds, since this may trigger massive blood loss; leave this to a vet.

Common ailments

Cats can contract a variety of illnesses, many of which can be treated successfully. You must seek veterinary advice and treatment quickly and faithfully follow instructions regarding medication and care. It will help the vet treat your cat more effectively if you can provide as many details as possible about your pet. This is where knowing your cat well can be, quite literally in some cases, a lifesaver. The checklist shows information you should provide to your vet.

Checklist
- ✓ your pet's symptoms
- ✓ when they started
- ✓ how long they have been present
- ✓ how your cat's usual behavior is affected

Feline influenza (feline respiratory disease/cat flu)

Flu in cats is not uncommon. In houses with more than one cat, and particularly in catteries, it can soon spread to other cats. Generally, the mortality rate in cats infected by cat flu is low.

Symptoms

These vary but may include loss of appetite, fever, sneezing, depression, inflamed or reddened eyes, yellow or thick green discharge from the nose, occasional coughing, and ulcers on the tongue.

Causes

The two main causes are viral. One is known as feline calicivirus (FCV). The other is known as feline herpes virus (FHV) or feline viral rhino-tracheitus (FVR). Either virus is transferred from the affected cat through aerosol droplets from sneezes. Unfortunately, some cats are carriers, and although they don't show any signs of flu, they can still pass it to other cats.

Drooling is a common symptom of cat flu.

What to do

Isolate an affected cat as soon as symptoms are noticed and contact the vet within 24 hours. The incubation period is 2 to 10 days, but even after successful treatment many cats are still carriers of the virus. In such cases, it is best if the affected cat is never allowed to come into contact with other cats. Vaccines—both injected under the skin and sprayed up the cat's nose—can provide some protection.

Treatment

There are two parts to treatment. The first is to nurse the cat to get him eating and drinking again, and the second is to administer drugs to alleviate his symptoms. The vet may prescribe antibiotics and mucolytics (which help clear the mucus from the respiratory system).

Halitosis (bad breath)

This is one of the most common mouth problems suffered by cats; most show symptoms before they are three years old.

Symptoms

Foul-smelling breath as well as tender gums, loss of appetite, and excessive drooling. Yellow-brown stains on the teeth where they meet the gums are signs of plaque and calculus (a buildup of minerals), which can lead to heart and kidney disease if not treated.

Causes

Usually gingivitis (inflammation of the gums) or food trapped between the teeth, which attracts bacteria. It is also a symptom of renal failure.

Rotten teeth and diseased gums are causes of bad breath (halitosis.)

What to do

Keep the cat's teeth in good condition. Regularly cleaning them can act as a preventive and as a way of inspecting the cat's teeth to find minor problems while they can still be dealt with. Take your cat for regular checkups, including a mouth examination.

Treatment

If your cat has gingivitis, it may be helpful to use an antiseptic spray in his mouth. Ask the vet for advice on this. Feeding mainly soft, wet food may adversely affect the teeth, so provide some crunchy food (kibble or biscuit-type feed) at every meal to help clean teeth. Feline "dental toys," if the cat will play with them, may also help to keep his teeth clean.

Vomiting

This is a symptom of an underlying condition, not an illness in itself.

Symptoms

A forceful expulsion of the contents of the cat's stomach and/or small intestine through the mouth.

Causes

These include:

• a sudden change in diet
• motion sickness
• heatstroke
• conditions that affect the chemical composition of the blood, such as diabetes, renal failure, liver disease, or a bacterial infection
• a foreign body in the stomach
• gastric dilation/torsion
• stomach cancer
• parasitic worms
• fear and stress
• trauma to the head
• infections
• ingestion of emetic substances, such as grass
• hairballs

What to do

If your cat suddenly and repeatedly vomits, you should withhold food and water and contact the vet. Keep the cat where you can see him and cover the floor with newspaper or something similar to keep your home clean. Note the times of vomiting and the consistency, color, and quantity of the vomit. By doing this, you will help the vet find the cause and therefore treat the problem effectively. Occasional vomiting is normal, and requires no action. In cases of recurring vomiting, or where large amounts of vomit are produced or there is blood in the vomit, seek veterinary advice.

Vomiting that you consider to be a result of your cat's scavenging, and

Vomiting may be caused by hairballs, but regular grooming will reduce the risk of these developing.

which is therefore intermittent and not severe, is best treated by fasting the cat for 24 hours. During this time, it's vital to regularly offer the cat small amounts of water to drink to help prevent dehydration.

After this time, reintroduce food with small, light meals, such as scrambled eggs or boiled chicken, gradually building up to his former feeding regimen. If the vomiting continues or starts again when food is reintroduced, seek veterinary advice as soon as possible.

You can help prevent some of the causes of vomiting by treating your cat on a regular basis for internal parasites (worms), discouraging him from scavenging, not making sudden changes to his diet, not feeding him prior to traveling, and not overfeeding him.

Treatment

In severe cases, it's not unusual for the affected cat to be placed on an intravenous drip to keep him hydrated. If a foreign body is wedged somewhere in the digestive system, surgery will be needed to remove it.

Diarrhea

Like vomiting, diarrhea is a symptom of an underlying condition and not an illness in itself.

Symptoms

Pungent, liquid-like feces; these may be passed frequently, necessitating many trips to the litter box, or appear as "accidents" around the house. If your cat has colitis (an inflammation of the colon), his feces will contain quite a lot of mucus and bright red blood.

Another symptom of colitis is tenesmus, where the cat strains to defecate; this is often mistaken for a symptom of constipation. Diarrhea often leads to dehydration, so your cat may appear slightly disoriented.

Causes

Diarrhea may simply be a symptom of overeating or stress. Intestinal worms are a common cause of diarrhea, as are foreign bodies in the digestive system and fungal infections.

What to do

Prevent the cat from eating anything, but be sure that he is given adequate amounts of drinking water. If the diarrhea is acute, provide the cat with a rehydrating fluid (see "First-aid kit" on page 157) and contact the vet.

Keep your cat where you can see him, covering the floor with newspapers or something similar to keep your home clean. Note the frequency of the diarrhea and the consistency, color, and quantity of the feces. By doing this, you will help the vet find the cause of the sudden diarrhea and treat the problem effectively.

Treatment

The treatment for diarrhea depends upon the underlying cause. If it is due to internal parasites, anthelmintics (wormers) will be used to rid the cat of the infestation, while antibiotics will be used for infections.

Diarrhea can cause the cat to dehydrate and can lead to irreparable body damage (particularly of the kidneys) and even death. In all cases of severe diarrhea (where overeating is not the cause), if it persists or there is blood in the feces, consult your vet immediately so the cat can be treated at once.

Enteritis

This is inflammation of the intestines, causing diarrhea.

Symptoms

Diarrhea and signs of blood in the loose stools may indicate this condition.

Causes

Enteritis is very common among young cats and can be caused by different things, but often it's the bacterium *Escherichia coli* (known as *E. coli*) that is the culprit. Another major cause of enteritis is campylobacter bacteria; in humans, "food poisoning" of this type is known as dysentery.

Diarrhea and the risk to humans

Diarrhea in your cat may be caused by a zoonotic disease—one that can be transmitted to humans. Such diseases include campylobacter and salmonella, both caused by harmful bacteria. To reduce the chance of any of these diseases being passed on to you and your family, always wash your hands after handling your cat, particularly before eating. Isolate the affected cat and keep him on water and electrolytes for 24 hours, dosing with kaolin solution (available from vets, doctors, and drugstores), about every 2 hours. After the fast, food intake should gradually be built up again; cooked chicken, rabbit, and fish are excellent foods for a recovering cat.

What to do
Observe your cat's actions and the amount, color, consistency, and smell of his stools. In particular, look for any signs of blood in the feces.

Treatment
Immediate treatment with a broad-spectrum antibiotic, together with regular doses of kaolin, may cure the condition. Sometimes more than one antibiotic is needed, or more than one course. Enteritis can be life-threatening, and treatment must start as soon as possible.

Constipation
Constipation comprises a failure by the cat to pass feces (or passing smaller amounts less frequently than usual). It is a symptom, not a disease, which may have many underlying causes, and is fairly common in elderly cats.

Symptoms
A cat producing extremely dry feces or straining to defecate is probably constipated. Each cat is different, but cats should be expected to defecate one to four times daily.

Causes
Any debilitating disease can cause constipation, as can a foreign body blocking the cat's digestive system (usually in the intestines). Constipation can also be a symptom of prostate problems in male cats.

What to do
Providing your cat with food high in fiber and giving a good overall balanced diet will often help prevent constipation.

Provide an incontinent cat with litter boxes throughout the house to reduce the risk of accidents.

Treatment
If an internal blockage is the cause, the cat will need surgery. In cases linked with diet, laxatives and a change of diet may be all that's needed. Constipation is potentially very dangerous, so always consult your vet when it occurs.

Urinary incontinence
This is the inability to control urination.

Symptoms
The cat has "accidents," particularly when resting. He doesn't urinate deliberately, but because of his condition, the urine dribbles out involuntarily, particularly when he is lying down.

Causes
There are many possible causes of urinary incontinence, which may include faulty urethral valves, congenital defects of the cat's urinary system, urolithiasis (crystals or "stones" of insoluble calcium in the urinary system), cancer, or prostate problems (in male cats). Urinary incontinence is seen particularly in older queens.

What to do
When taking your cat for veterinary examination, provide a fresh sample of his urine for testing; this will reveal if any diseases are causing the problem. It's unfair to punish or reproach a cat for incontinence. The cat's bed is likely to become soiled, so bedding must be changed regularly, preferably daily.

Treatment
Surgery may be needed to treat faulty urethral valves, congenital defects, urolithiasis, cancer, or prostate problems, while drug therapy may be used to improve the effectiveness of the urethra in preventing urine leakage. Urinary incontinence is not life-threatening in itself, but because some of the possible underlying causes may be serious, it's better to seek veterinary advice sooner rather than later.

Arthritis
This causes inflammation of the joints. There are two forms of arthritis that may affect cats, osteoarthritis and traumatic arthritis.

Symptoms
Swollen joints, difficulty in walking, and lameness.

Causes

Osteoarthritis may be a condition in itself or a result of other conditions. It is a progressive and painful disease that will seriously affect the cat's quality of life. It may affect one or more joints, and the seriousness of the condition will depend on which joints are involved and the general health of the cat.

Osteoarthritis is not nearly as common in cats as it is in dogs, but overweight cats are more prone to osteoarthritis. Traumatic arthritis is a direct result of an injury to the joint; for example, it may be the result of being hit by a car or a sprain while exercising.

What to do

Your vet will advise you on what action you should take, depending on the underlying causes and treatment being given.

Treatment

The treatment for arthritis may include anti-inflammatory drugs and painkillers, and in some cases surgery may be needed. All cases of osteoarthritis should be treated seriously. Don't wait until your cat is unable to walk before consulting the vet.

A physical examination and observation of the cat's movement, along with X-rays and analysis of joint fluid, will give the vet an indication of how serious an arthritic problem is.

Poor exercise tolerance

Sometimes a normally active cat will develop problems that make exercise difficult for him.

Symptoms

Pain and discomfort during what should be normal exercise.

Causes

This is often a direct result of inflammation of the joints (arthritis). When a muscle is diseased (for example, from a bacterial infection), it is referred to as myopathy; when a muscle is inflamed, it is referred to as myositis.

What to do

Be very careful about administering painkillers, unless according to veterinary instructions. Painkillers can easily lull a cat into a false sense of security, causing him to use injured joints and resulting in more damage.

Treatment

In cases of mild myopathy, for example, where your cat develops a slight limp for 24 to 36 hours, simply resting him will probably relieve the problem (sometimes it's necessary to confine him to a limited space, such as a pen). If the limp persists beyond this time, seek veterinary advice and treatment. When a joint is damaged, the injury is referred to as a sprain and may involve damage to cartilage and/or ligaments. While not dangerous in itself, the condition is painful. If not treated adequately, a sprain may lead to osteoarthritis, and the damage is usually permanent.

Cloudy or opaque eyes indicate a vision problem; many cats adjust remarkably well to being blind in one or both eyes.

Blindness

This may mean limited vision or total lack of vision.

Symptoms

Your cat may bump into furniture and other objects for no apparent reason. It's also quite common for an elderly cat to have more problems with his eyesight in bright light and in darkness, and he may be reluctant to venture out at such times.

Causes

There is a variety of causes, from injury to hereditary conditions. As cats age, it is quite common for a bluish color to appear in the eyes as the lens deteriorates.

What to do

Symptoms of failing eyesight should be taken to a vet without delay.

Treatment

This depends upon the cause, but many cases of total blindness are untreatable.

Feline chlamydial infection

Chlamydia consists of infection with *Chlamydia psittaci*, a bacterium that causes conjunctivitis.

Symptoms

Conjunctivitis (reddened eyes) and a thick discharge from the eyes. Sneezing and nasal discharge are also common.

Causes

Cats become infected by *Chlamydia psittaci*, which is spread by other infected cats in their bodily discharges.

What to do

Seek immediate veterinary treatment for any eye infection.

Treatment

The vet will prescribe antibiotics, and the whole course must be completed. If feline chlamydial infection is not treated quickly and adequately, it can spread to the gastrointestinal (digestive) and genital systems of the cat and may cause reproductive problems in queens.

Ear mites

These are insect parasites very common in cats.

Symptoms

Persistent ear scratching. A buildup of wax in the ears, dotted with black specks, is an indication that a cat may have ear mites; the black specks are probably spots of dried blood. The mites can move down the ear canal and infect the middle ear; such an

Feline chlamydial infection, common in kittens of one to nine months, causes conjunctivitis.

infection will cause the affected animal to lose his sense of balance. The cat may be unable to hold his head straight or, in more serious cases, may constantly fall over.

Causes

Ear mites (*Otodectes cynotis*), which are common in cats and wild rodents.

What to do

Seek veterinary advice in all cases of ear mites, or if your cat has a loss of balance. All animals who have been in contact with the infested cat must also be treated, since ear mites can infest other animals, who may not show any symptoms for some time.

Treatment

In mild cases, the vet will prescribe ear drops and possibly anti-inflammatory

If left untreated, the irritation caused by ear mites will cause the cat to scratch, sometimes until his ears actually bleed.

drugs for irritation. Mites are easily treated if caught early enough. The mites are usually white or colorless and aren't visible to the naked eye; a magnifying glass or otoscope (a special instrument used to inspect the insides of the ears) is needed. Sometimes the mites aren't visible even with an otoscope, since they hide under pieces of earwax.

Ear canker (otitis)

An inflammation of the skin lining the ear, otitis is one of the most common conditions in cats and may occur in one or both ears.

Symptoms

These may include regular ear scratching and head shaking, a discharge or smell from the ear, and reddening of the inner ear flap and/or the ear hole. The cat may hiss at anyone who tries to touch him around the ear.

Causes

Normally, the amount of wax

produced in a cat's ear is exactly the same amount that is lost naturally. Much of it is lost through evaporation of water from the wax. Problems occur when the ears don't get proper ventilation and the wax builds up. This excess wax causes irritation, and the ear is stimulated to produce even more wax. This leads to ideal conditions for normally harmless fungi and bacteria to grow and prosper. Ear mites, foreign bodies in the ear, and skin problems can also cause otitis.

What to do

Take a cat who shows any symptoms of irritated ears to the vet as soon as possible—immediately if you suspect a foreign body is lodged in the ear. *Never* attempt to remove a blockage yourself, or you may damage the cat's ear permanently. Don't put any liquid, ointment, or other medication inside the cat's ears unless instructed by your vet, and don't attempt to put any solid object inside the cat's ear, including cotton swabs, which may also cause damage.

Discharge from the ear should not be cleaned up until your vet has had a chance to see it, since it may provide some clues about the ear problem.

Treatment

Treatment may include syringing of the ear or application of a topical medicine, such as ear drops or ointment. Whatever medications are prescribed, it's important that you administer them exactly as instructed and always finish the course of treatment.

In serious cases of recurring otitis, surgery may be necessary to improve ear ventilation. Even though otitis is not a serious condition, if not properly treated, it can become chronic, causing severe problems and possibly damaging parts of the ear and the cat's hearing.

Ear-flap wounds

These are scratches or tears in the ear flaps (pinnas).

Symptoms

Any ear wound, no matter how minor, is likely to bleed a great deal. Even if the wound doesn't cause the cat any real pain, the irritation of blood running down the ear is likely to cause him to scratch at his ear and shake his head.

Causes

Ear flaps are often bitten and scratched during fights, and some felines, particularly farm cats, may injure their ear flaps in their usual day-to-day life.

What to do

With someone restraining the cat, clean the wounds with saline solution. Once they're cleaned, it will be possible to see the extent of the damage; if it's significant, seek veterinary treatment, since the injuries may need to be sutured.

Treatment

After cleaning with saline solution, cover minor wounds with antiseptic ointment, cream, or powder. If the wounds look inflamed within a few days of the injury, consult the vet, since antibiotic treatment may be required.

Kidney (renal) failure

Kidney failure is probably the most common problem seen in elderly cats. It is also a symptom of polycystic kidney disease (PKD), a hereditary condition often found in Persian cats.

Symptoms

These include a seemingly insatiable thirst, passing large amounts of urine either all at once or at very frequent intervals, vomiting, diarrhea, loss of appetite, weight loss, halitosis, and anemia.

If ear-flap wounds aren't treated, they may become infected and far more serious.

Due to the long-term nature of the intensive treatment required for renal failure, veterinary costs will be high.

Causes

For various reasons, including infections and physical damage, the nephrons (parts of the kidneys that remove waste products from the blood) fail to do their job properly, and this leads to chronic renal failure.

This is an extremely serious and usually irreversible condition with a very poor chance of recovery. It rarely occurs in cats under five years of age.

What to do

Renal failure is life-threatening. Don't hesitate to contact the vet if you suspect this condition in your cat.

Treatment

Treatment of an affected cat may include a period of intensive care during which the cat will have fluids administered via an intravenous drip, plus a special diet coupled with a restful lifestyle and a prescribed course of medication. A cat with renal failure will die, and you may choose to euthanize him.

Feline distemper (feline enteritis)

Also called feline panleukopenia, this widespread, life-threatening viral disease attacks the white blood cells and the cat's gut.

Symptoms

These include loss of appetite and persistent vomiting and/or diarrhea.

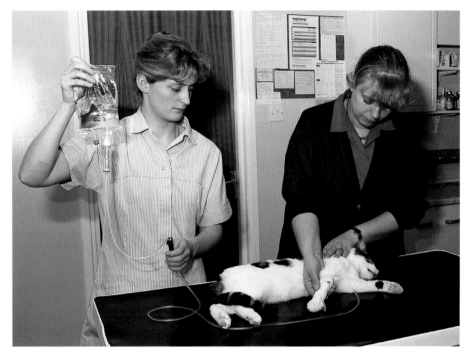

Causes

The virus is passed from an infected cat to others by direct or indirect contact.

What to do

This disease is highly infectious, so isolate any infected cats. To guard against it, make sure your cat is vaccinated and receives regular boosters.

Treatment

There is no real treatment for distemper, but special care and intensive nursing may alleviate the symptoms. Seek immediate veterinary treatment for any cat showing symptoms. A severe infection may kill a young cat or kitten very quickly.

Diabetes mellitus

In this hormonal condition, the cat is unable to control his blood sugar levels.

Symptoms

Increased appetite, particularly if coupled with other symptoms, such as an increase in the amount of urine passed, lethargy, weight loss, and perhaps cataracts. Very often, symptoms of diabetes mellitus are seen in queens just after they have started estrus.

Many of the conditions associated with diabetes mellitus are also common symptoms of other, less serious diseases or other factors. For example, increased thirst may simply be due to your cat being fed a dry diet.

Causes

A lack of insulin (produced by the pancreas) or an increase in blood sugar levels (hyperglycemia). It is most common in cats over eight years of age.

Due to the increased levels of progesterone (a hormone) in the blood during phantom or pseudo pregnancies, unspayed queens are said to be more than three times more susceptible to diabetes mellitus, and obese cats of either sex are also at increased risk.

What to do

Take any cat showing symptoms of diabetes for examination by a vet as soon as possible.

Treatment

Since treatment for this condition is likely to be long-term and include regular insulin injections and other treatment, the costs in terms of both time and money will be fairly high.

Typically, you will need to collect and test a sample of urine from your cat every morning to check the glucose levels, calculate the amount of insulin needed and administer it by injection, and feed your cat an extremely regulated (high-fiber) diet at specific times. Your vet will advise you on all of these matters. In queens, spaying will keep the cat's condition stable.

Diabetes insipidus

This condition renders the body incapable of regulating the use of water.

Symptoms

These include polydipsia (excessive thirst) and polyuria (production of large amounts of urine).

Causes

Diabetes insipidus is caused by lack of the anti-diuretic hormone ADH (produced in the cat's pituitary gland), or failure of the kidneys to respond to this hormone.

Normally, the production of ADH is increased when there is little water intake and decreased when the cat drinks large quantities of water, thus controlling the body's water balance.

What to do

Any sign of abnormal water intake should be investigated by a vet as soon as possible.

Treatment

Depending on which form of diabetes inspidus is present, treatment may involve administering ADH to the affected cat via nose drops.

Abnormal water intake

This is an increased or decreased need to drink water.

Symptoms

The cat drinks either more or less water than is normal for him. Other symptoms include an increased or decreased need to urinate.

Voracious hunger can sometimes be an indication of diabetes mellitus.

Causes

It can be a symptom of cystitis, tapeworm infestation, diabetes insipidus, or diabetes mellitus.

What to do

Keep an eye on urine deposits in the litter box; if you know what is generally normal for your pet, then a change will be detected early. Cystitis is indicated by discomfort and straining to urinate, while tapeworm infestation is signaled by the visible presence of worms in feces and tiny white segments of them sticking to fur around the anus.

Treatment

Take your cat to the vet; treatment will depend on the cause of the condition. If tapeworms are to blame, worming will be in order, while cystitis is treatable with antibiotics.

Increased thirst can be due to a cat being fed a dry diet.

Feline leukemia

This viral infection affects the cat's immune system.

Symptoms

Lethargy, high temperature, lack of appetite and enlarged lymph nodes in the neck, armpits, and groin.

Causes

The feline leukemia virus (FeLV), which is present in blood, semen, and saliva; it is spread through mating and bite wounds.

What to do

There can be a delay of as much as three years between the time the cat becomes infected and when he shows signs of the condition, so there is no real urgency to seek veterinary treatment unless the cat exhibits severe symptoms that cause him pain or discomfort.

Treatment

There is no cure for FeLV. Many cats infected with the disease make a reasonable recovery naturally but then become carriers, spreading the condition to other cats with whom they come into contact. If you have more than one cat in your home, the vet may recommend that the infected cat be euthanized in order to limit the risk of the infection spreading to others.

If you have just one cat, you must not allow him to go outside, where he may come into contact with, and therefore infect, other cats in your neighborhood. Some owners prefer not to take the chance that their cat will infect others and choose to have him euthanized.

There is a vaccine available for this condition; ask your vet about having your cat immunized.

Feline infectious peritonitis (FIP)

Caused by a virus that affects cats under about three years of age, FIP is known to spread rapidly among cats and is particularly dangerous in multiple-cat households.

Symptoms

These include loss of appetite, a swollen abdomen, weight loss, breathing problems, and a fever.

Causes

A virus (feline coronavirus), which is passed from an infected cat to others by direct or indirect contact.

What to do

Isolate infected cats and seek immediate veterinary advice.

Treatment

There is no treatment for FIP, and most cats die as a direct result of this infection. It may be advisable to euthanize your cat; your vet will help you to make this decision.

Bites sustained in fights are a common means by which FeLV is transferred from one cat to another.

Feline immune deficiency

Also known as feline AIDS, this viral infection affects the RNA (ribonucleic acid) that is involved in the manufacture of proteins within the cat's cells. It prevents the body's immune system from fighting off infections.

Symptoms

This condition allows many infections to become established in the affected cat but has no symptoms as such.

Causes

The feline immunodeficiency virus (FIV) multiplies in the white cells in the cat's blood and is often transmitted through cat bites.

What to do

You must take any cat suspected of having an FIV infection to the vet. Infected cats are susceptible to chronic long-term illnesses, weight loss, and other debilitating conditions as a result of the infections caused by the lack of immune response.

Treatment

There is no cure for FIV infection. Like humans with AIDS, however, cats can harbor the virus for some time before becoming sick. In a safe indoor environment with proper nutrition and care, a cat who has been diagnosed (by a blood test) but isn't symptomatic can live for months or even years in good health. The risk to other cats in the household is small as long as there's no aggressive fighting among the pets. Once the infected cat becomes ill, immune suppression makes repeated illnesses likely, with episodes becoming progressively more severe. At that point, euthanasia is usually recommended.

Obesity

This problem is not confined to the human population—many owners overfeed and underexercise their pets, sometimes with the best of intentions.

Symptoms

The cat is overweight, even grossly fat, signified by rolls of fat under the skin. This can cause breathlessness and a reluctance to exercise. It can predispose the cat to joint problems and other illnesses associated with obesity, such as failure of the heart and other organs.

Old cats are prone to obesity if they are not very active.

Causes

Old age, when the cat doesn't exercise as much as he once may have; overeating; or being fed an unsuitable diet.

What to do

Consult your vet regarding a suitable diet plan.

Treatment

Encourage your cat to exercise more by playing, and hide his food ration around the house so he has to hunt for it, thereby expending energy. Follow your vet's diet plan strictly; if the cat is old, a specially formulated low-calorie diet for elderly felines will probably be recommended.

Heatstroke

This is a fever caused by the failure of the body's temperature-regulating mechanism when exposed to excessively high temperatures.

Symptoms

Agitation and extreme distress. First, the cat will stretch out and pant heavily, then drool and stagger as if drunk. Finally, if untreated, he will collapse, go into a coma, and die.

Causes

Usually due to being left in a car or taking a long trip in one. If the car is poorly ventilated, the temperature rises to a dangerous level quickly, even in the cooler sunshine of spring or autumn.

What to do

You must act fast. For mildly affected cats, simply moving them to a cool

Cats will naturally seek shelter from the sun or move to a cooler area of the house when they feel they are getting too hot.

place and ensuring a steady passage of cool air will usually be sufficient.

Treatment
In bad cases, cool the cat down with cold water from a hose (using a fine misting spray) or by gently pouring bowlfuls of cold water over him. In very bad cases, cover the cat with wet towels, including the head (but keep the nose and mouth clear) and keep dousing him with cold water. You should seek veterinary assistance immediately.

In all cases of heatstroke, it is vital to keep the head cool, as the brain may literally be cooked, and brain death can occur.

Flea dermatitis
This is irritation and soreness of the skin around flea bites.

Symptoms
Red, raw areas and scabs caused by the cat scratching himself obsessively; these may be found all over the cat's body or just in localized areas such as near the base of the tail and behind the ears. Some cats are more sensitive than others to flea bites and can be driven almost to distraction by the itching.

Causes
A reaction to the saliva of the fleas when they bite the cat in order to feed on his blood.

What to do
Consult your vet.

Treatment
The cat may require a course of treatment to alleviate irritation, along with treatment to kill the fleas and prevent reinfestation.

Ringworm
This is a fungal infection of the skin.

Symptoms
Scratching and circular areas of hair loss, with the visible skin becoming scaly and raised around the edges of the lesions.

Causes
Fungi, including *Microsporum canis*, *Microsporum gypseum* and *Trichophyton mentagrophytes*. Spores of these fungi may be wind-borne or found in the soil.

What to do
Some of the fungi responsible for ringworm are zoonotic (contractable by humans), so take care that you and your family are not infected. Only your vet can prescribe effective treatment, so seek advice right away.

Treatment
Washing the cat with a fungicidal product prescribed by a vet will help kill the fungi. Topical applications of fungicide may also be recommended.

Telltale signs of ringworm infection include a circular area of hair loss and scaly, flaking skin.

Complementary therapies

More and more vets are now adopting a natural approach when treating sick animals, cats included. Natural medicine denotes the use of complementary (natural and traditional) therapies and remedies, as opposed to conventional medicine (synthetic drugs and remedies). A more holistic view is taken of ailments whereby the whole animal is considered rather than simply the condition(s) that he is exhibiting. Diagnosis takes into account everything on the checklist.

Checklist

- ✓ overall physical health
- ✓ mental health
- ✓ environment
- ✓ exercise
- ✓ daily routine
- ✓ companionship
- ✓ nutrition (food and water)
- ✓ hygiene

What is involved?

Once the vet or practitioner has ascertained what is ailing your cat and why, he will decide upon the appropriate action or treatment. In some cases, the treatment may simply involve making improvements in your cat's living environment or exercise levels or changing his diet to one that is better suited to his digestive system. In other instances, it may be that a course of treatment—acupuncture, for example—may have the desired effect in curing whatever is wrong. Sometimes extra companionship, either human or that of another animal, can have the desired effect of alleviating health problems that are related to anxiety or stress.

Do they work?

Many people and vets believe and advocate that they do, and they can recount innumerable case histories showing how natural medicine triumphed where conventional treatment failed. There appears to be little scientific research to substantiate such claims where some therapies are concerned (such as spiritual healing and feng shui), but these remedies have been used for a long time, even thousands of years, and something that doesn't work is unlikely to remain in use. With most forms of complementary therapy, as long as they are applied with expertise and knowledge, the worst that can happen is that they have no effect.

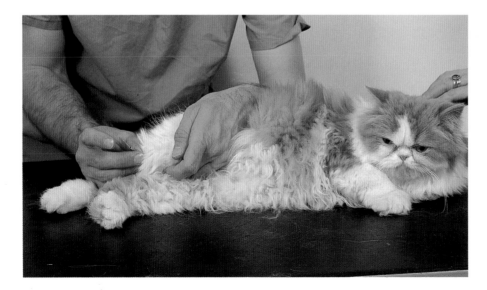

Acupuncture has been used for thousands of years to treat a variety of ailments, both animal and human.

Top tip

Complementary therapies should not be considered the last resort by pet owners but as viable forms of treatment that are well worth trying. The range of ailments and conditions that can benefit from natural therapies is vast. A small selection of these includes poisoning, diabetes mellitus, osteoarthritis, gingivitis, constipation, cancer, nervousness, aggression, skin diseases, internal and external parasites, and anal gland disorders. Ask your vet's advice for practitioners in your area.

When to try them

Complementary therapies are so called because most of them are complementary to each other, and many of them can be in conjunction with conventional medicine. Better results or speedier recoveries can sometimes be obtained by using a combination of two or more therapies to treat a health problem, depending on what the problem is.

Finding a practitioner

An increasing number of vets are using natural healing treatments, so it shouldn't be too difficult to find an experienced and trustworthy practitioner. Even if your own vet doesn't practice traditional medicine in the particular field you are interested in, he may be able to refer you to a reputable person who does. The Internet is another valuable resource for finding a practitioner.

Frequently asked question

Correctly administered, complementary therapies have been known to bring about seemingly miraculous results.

Q My vet is quite old-fashioned and won't entertain the idea of any form of "alternative" treatment, but now I would like my cat to be treated naturally wherever possible. What should I do?

A If your vet won't refer you to a complementary practitioner, it may be advisable to take your business to a veterinary clinic that will. You are quite within your rights to do so; after all, it's your cat's health that is important, not the feelings of your vet. Contact veterinary practices in your area—or farther afield if you have no other choice—to find one that suits you and your cat's needs. Bear in mind, though, that the farther you have to travel, the less convenient it may be in an emergency.

AT-A-GLANCE COMPLEMENTARY THERAPIES

THERAPY	WHAT IT INVOLVES
Acupressure	Noninvasive pressure is applied to specific points (acupoints) on the body by the practitioner's fingers or thumbs to induce the same reactions in the patient as acupuncture.
Acupuncture	Fine copper or steel needles are inserted in the skin at acupoints on the body to relieve illness and mental and/or physical stress. This treatment has been shown to alleviate pain, heal damage, promote body chemicals that produce a sense of well-being, improve the appetite, and raise energy levels.
Aromatherapy	Essential plant oils—diluted, undiluted, or mixed with a bland base oil as appropriate—are used to treat ailments. They are used either by allowing the cat to choose and smell certain oils as his body dictates or by applying them topically (to the surface of his skin) where appropriate. They can be used for a whole host of complaints, from fleas to emotional problems.
Biochemical tissue salts	A form of homeopathy (see opposite) using 12 energized mineral salts.
Chiropractic	A manipulative method of treating disorders and displacements of joints, especially those in the spine. It can prove useful in cases of back pain, lameness, and joint injuries.
Color therapy	Colors have an effect on physical and mental well-being, so they can be used to treat a variety of ailments.
Crystals and gems	Through energy waves, each type of crystal can help heal mental and physical ailments. Once the symptoms have been determined, the practitioner chooses appropriate stones for the cat to wear, have around his body while resting, and/or have in his bed.
Dowsing	Although not a treatment in itself, it is used to diagnose ailments by means of a divining rod or pendulum held over the cat.
Electro-crystal therapy	This enhances the effects of crystals through an energy field created by a small electric charge. Special equipment is used to administer this painless treatment.
Feng shui	This ancient Chinese art involves arranging your cat's home environment to optimize his mental and physical well-being. Acupuncture was derived from this practice.
Flower remedies	These are essences derived from specific flower petals that have been floated in water to transfer their healing properties into the liquid, to which a tiny amount of alcohol (usually brandy) has been added to preserve them. Essences are available for all sorts of behavior problems, including anxiety, aggression, timidity, and shock. They appear also to alleviate physical ailments if they are linked to mental or emotional problems.
Herbalism	Plant-based natural medicines for both external and internal use. For example, the willow tree is a source of a chemical similar to salicylic acid (aspirin), while digitalis (heart medicine) is derived from foxglove. An infusion of mallow can be used to bathe swollen areas to reduce swelling, while comfrey can be taken internally to help repair bone fractures.

THERAPY	WHAT IT INVOLVES
Homeopathy	Remedies are derived from animal, mineral, and vegetable substances through a special process called "potentization" that releases their therapeutic properties. It works on the principle of "like cures like": If a substance causes adverse symptoms in an animal, a minute "energized" dose of it can also cure those symptoms. Remedies include those from seemingly strange sources such as lead, poisonous snake venom, arsenic, egg yolk, and animal tissue, among many others.
Iridology	Ailments are diagnosed by examining the iris of the eye; minute changes in its color and shape can inform the practitioner about the cat's health status, the location and type of disease present in the body, and whether he will have a tendency toward disease in the future.
Kinesiology	Testing muscles that relate to an organ system through an energy field (the cat) to determine imbalances.
Magnotherapy	The use of magnets to promote healing by increasing blood supply to the afflicted area.
Osteopathy	Manipulative adjustment of muscles and joints to relieve misalignment that is causing pain.
Physiotherapy	Body manipulation, massage, exercise, specialized machines (such as ultrasound), and the application of warmth or cold as appropriate to help treat disease, injury, or deformity.
Radionics	This distance healing works by the practitioner assessing a "witness" (a lock of hair, for example) from the cat to determine what ails him, then directing healing energy vibrations at him through a specialized radionics instrument known as the "black box."
Reflexology	Diseases of body organs are treated by applying pressure to particular joints.
Spiritual (faith) healing	The "laying-on of hands" on the animal or the affected body part; healing powers are directed at the patient through the healer. This form of healing has proven effective with "incurable" diseases such as cancer, though is not guaranteed to work; it depends on the individual cat.
Touch massage	Gentle, repetitive massaging movements, which are said to generate specific brain wave patterns in the recipient that help promote mental and physical healing.

TWILIGHT YEARS

The company of an aging cat in good health is delightful, soothing, and just as rewarding as playing with a kitten. To care for an older cat, you may need to make a few changes in his everyday routine, making a few allowances for his age, but it will be well worth the effort.

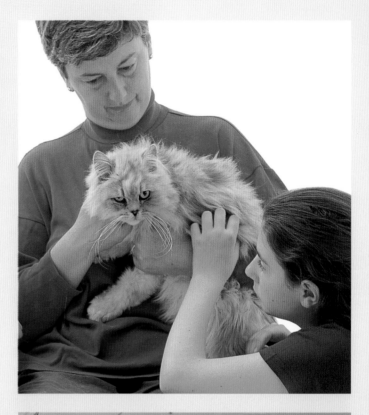

Caring for your senior cat

A cat can be considered old when he starts to take things easy and spends more time than usual sleeping. The old cat's reactions are still sharp, his movements are subtle, and he may even deign to chase string and pat feathers, as long as he is not made to feel foolish. Just because he sits around a lot and is undemanding and quiet, an elderly cat should not be ignored. To remain happy and in the best possible health, he needs everything on the checklist.

Checklist

✓ lots of love and affection
✓ particular attention to claws and teeth
✓ extra attention to diet
✓ help with grooming
✓ twice-yearly veterinary checkups
✓ patience and understanding if "accidents" occur
✓ unchanging daily routine
✓ minimal upheaval in his life
✓ plenty of sleep

Lifestyle

Just like elderly people, old cats are resistant to and can be upset by major changes in their routine and lifestyle. If changes are necessary, try to incorporate them gradually to allow your cat time to get used to them. Everything should be done to keep the elderly cat feeling as good as possible. (For holiday tips, see pages 116–19.)

Disturbed behavior patterns may be the result of chronic illness in the old cat. For example, a previously clean cat may have "accidents" on chairs and carpets. If this happens, it may be best to keep the cat in areas of the house where such accidents don't matter—but that doesn't mean he should be shut away or limited in his access to his family, which would be unfair and cruel. It would also be unfair

Very old cats doze most of their days away and prefer to be where they are most comfortable, feel safe, and can relax and sleep deeply.

and cruel to chastise or ban the cat from the house for something that is beyond his control. Carpets can be replaced, but loving companions cannot.

Companionship

Some people consider getting a kitten when their established cat gets old. This can be a good or bad decision, depending on the temperament and nature of the aged cat. If he likes the kitten, he may gain a new lease on life. If he doesn't, he may resent the newcomer and become depressed and withdrawn, stop eating, and ultimately become very ill. If the old cat is the only one in the household and has always been a loner, it would be kinder not to get another cat or kitten.

If your elderly cat displays an increased need for your company, always give him plenty of attention and reassurance; you might even consider moving his bed into your bedroom at night if necessary. Leaving a radio on low while you are out can help provide "company."

Diet

Foods specially formulated for elderly cats are available, and these contain all the nutrients the aging body needs to remain in the best possible condition and help delay or alleviate the onset of conditions such as senility. Because older cats can often have urinary tract problems, a totally dry diet may not be the best choice; it may be wise to

Older cats are more prone to constipation, so watch for this and seek veterinary attention if it occurs.

consult your vet regarding the best type of food for your cat. See also "Feeding" on pages 38–45.

Bad teeth and inflamed gums are not uncommon in old cats; at this stage, your cat will find soft moist or semi-moist food easier to eat. Be sure there is always a plentiful supply of fresh, clean water.

A cat tends to slow down as he ages and may tend toward obesity if you don't monitor his diet closely.

Frequently asked question

Q How do you determine a cat's age in human years?

A By the time a kitten is 12 months old, he is thought to be the equivalent of a 15-year-old human and is considered physically mature, depending on his breed and type; 14 months equates to 18 years; 2 years is equivalent to 24 years. From then on, to calculate his approximate age in human years, add 4 years for every year that your cat lives. For example, a 10-year-old cat would be 56 in human years, and a 16-year-old would be 80.

LEFT *Because their bodies don't regulate temperature as efficiently as those of their younger counterparts, older cats seek out warm places to rest—on top of a dryer being a favorite spot. They also prefer to stay indoors when it's cold or wet outside.*

BELOW *Keep an eye on senior cats when they are allowed outside, particularly senile, blind, or deaf pets, who may get lost or face potential hazards from predators and traffic.*

Feline facts

• Unless you know his birth date, it is extremely difficult to age a mature, fit, and active cat aged between 3 and 13 accurately, because there are no specific signs of aging to look for, and cats age much more gracefully than their canine counterparts.

• On average, cats now live to about 14, thanks to improved geriatric feline veterinary care and nutrition. Many cats live until their late teens in reasonable health, although at this age they can look a little unkempt.

An older cat may not be able to defend his food as well as he once could, so if you have other cats and/or dogs, be sure they are not allowed to steal his meals or intimidate him while he is eating and scare him off.

Being less active as he grows older, it is easy for the cat to pile on weight, which can put undue strain on his heart and joints; keep a careful watch on this. He could also lose weight rapidly and starve if he isn't eating for some reason. Weighing your cat once a week can help you monitor his weight, and this is quite simple to do. First, weigh yourself on your bathroom scale, then weigh yourself again while holding the cat; deduct the first result from the second to ascertain your pet's weight. It may be easier for a helper to read the scale while you hold the cat.

Common ailments

As a cat ages, his body tissue starts to degenerate. This is inevitable and can't be prevented, although with care from both owner and vet, the effects can be eased. Old cats are prone to a number of particular ailments:

- claw wounds, due to a decreasing ability to retract them
- coat and skin complaints, due to inefficient grooming
- cold-related problems, due to decreased body temperature regulation
- constipation, due to decreased digestive efficiency
- deafness
- heart disease
- high blood pressure (hypertension)
- incontinence
- increased predisposition to hairballs
- injury, due to decrease in agility
- joint stiffness and arthritis
- kidney disease
- liver failure
- loss of appetite
- obesity-related problems
- senility
- sight problems
- tooth and gum problems

Seek veterinary advice for all of these ailments; the more quickly they are dealt with, the more likely it is that the treatment will be successful and your cat's comfortable life prolonged.

Excessive drinking can indicate a urinary problem that may need immediate veterinary treatment.

Time to say good-bye

Eventually, the older cat sleeps more and more and is increasingly reluctant to exercise. He may drink lots of fluids but take little food. While he is able to function normally, if only in this modified way, he is probably quite contented. If his bladder and bowels begin to fail and he is unable to eat, you must seek veterinary advice, for the only humane thing to do in these circumstances is to have the old cat put to sleep, allowing him to die painlessly and with dignity. It is the last kind thing you can do for a much-loved companion and friend. (See pages 186–189 for information on bereavement and euthanasia.)

Top tip

The key to good health care for your old cat lies in vigilance. Twice-yearly checkups by a vet will reveal early signs of problems; some vets run clinics for older cats, recognizing the need to spend a little extra time on these much-cherished companions. Extra attention should be given to grooming the old cat, since he may find grooming difficult if he is stiff or has arthritis—especially in hard-to-reach places, such as the back, back of the neck, and under the tail. Claws may need trimming regularly if the cat is not keeping them worn down through outdoor exercise or using a scratching post.

Bereavement

When a companion animal dies, or his death is imminent, this often has a huge impact on the humans who loved and cared for him. Losing a much-loved pet is just the same for many owners as coping with the death of a family member or close friend. Individual people deal with this trauma in different ways, but all or some of the stages of grief that are often encountered are shown on the checklist.

Checklist

✓ anticipation of loss
✓ shock
✓ denial
✓ anger
✓ depression
✓ acceptance

Why pet cats die

There are two reasons for a cat's death:

• sudden death through accident or illness
• euthanasia (being "put to sleep" or "put down") following an accident or because of old age or illness, when a cure is not possible and the cat's quality of life is or will be poor

In the first case, you will not be prepared for your pet's death, and it will no doubt come as a huge shock. In the second case, you can prepare for the inevitable, although it does not make it any easier to bear. Many owners blame

If you know your cat well, you'll know when the time has come to let him go with dignity and minimal discomfort.

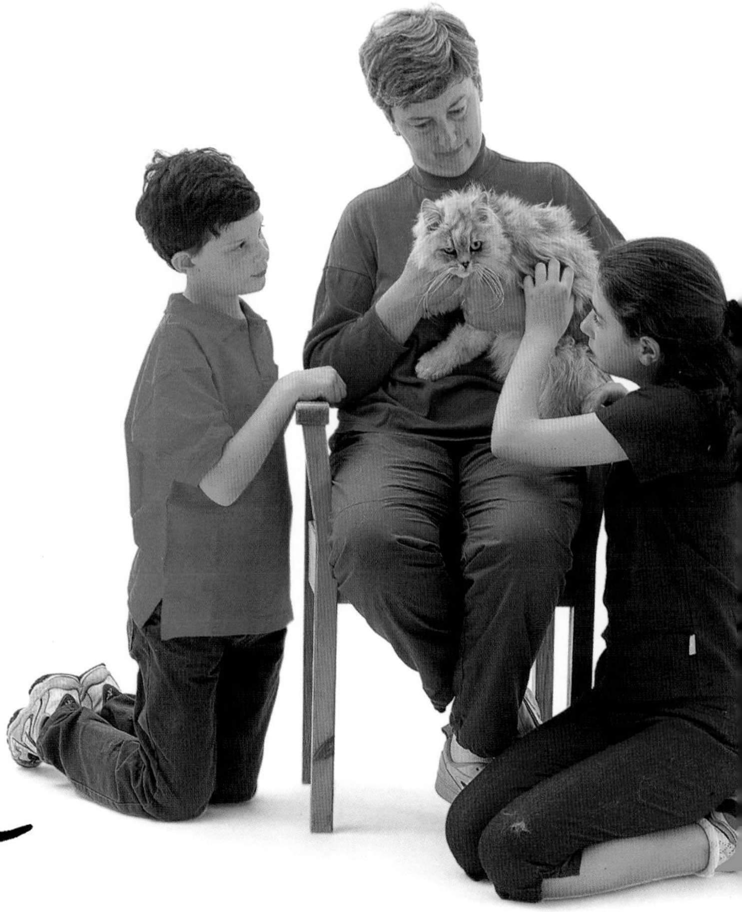

Feline fact

Sometimes, understandably, owners can't bear to lose a pet and delay having him put down, even when it really should be done. As a caring owner, you should put your pet's needs first, however hard it may be for you. If your cat is suffering, euthanasia is the kindest thing you can do for him. You can take comfort in knowing that all through his life, even at its end, you showed him love and compassion.

themselves for a pet's death and agonize over whether it could have been prevented if they had done things differently. This is a normal reaction, but sadly, it can't change what has happened. The important thing, for your sake, is to focus on the many happy times you enjoyed with your cherished pet and to treasure those memories.

Euthanasia

Other than sudden death, having a cat "put down" is the most humane way for him to die. A prolonged natural death can be traumatic for both pet and owner, as well as painful for the cat. While the process may be upsetting to read about, it can help to understand the process of euthanasia.

Talk it over with your vet first and decide whether having it done at home or at the vet clinic would be more suitable and practical. Also discuss the options of what to do with your pet's body. Once this has been mutually agreed, arrange a date, preferably sooner rather than later, so your pet's suffering, as well as your own, isn't prolonged.

At the veterinary clinic

Arrange a time when the vet clinic is likely to be quiet or you can enter and leave through a private entrance so that you don't have to face a crowded waiting room. Have a supportive person drive you there and back; you may well be upset and therefore in no fit state to drive yourself. Take a blanket in which to wrap your pet to bring him home again, if this is what you want to do.

Make the journey there as smooth, stress-free, and quiet as possible. If you will be able to bear up in your pet's last moments, then be with him. If you feel you will go to pieces, ask your vet and the vet nurse to deal with it; if you are terribly distressed, it may make your pet equally so, and his passing may not be as peaceful as it should be.

At home

This is more expensive but may be the preferred option if you are unable to get to the clinic, your cat is too ill to move, he finds travel upsetting, or you would prefer euthanasia to be done in familiar and comfortable surroundings. Request that a veterinary nurse attend, as well as the vet. The former can help out as required or where necessary and help keep you and the cat calm so the process is as stress-free as possible.

Did you know...?

Being animal lovers themselves, many vets find euthanizing pets as painful as the owners do (especially if the pet is well known to them), although it doesn't keep them from being professional about it. Just because vets may appear to be detached about the process doesn't mean that they don't care; they do, but they have to remain strong for the animals'—and often the owners'—sake. Many vets are now more aware of the fact that owners suffer great emotional pain when they lose a pet, and they are better equipped to cope with this than they may have been years ago. Because of this, they offer a much more sympathetic and caring service.

On the day, keep your cat's routine as usual, but give him lots of extra attention and cuddles if he will allow you to. He may not understand why you are being extra affectionate but may appreciate it nonetheless. It will make you feel better as well as make the most of those last precious moments.

The process

Properly carried out, euthanasia is quick and relatively painless. The vet may administer a sedative injection if the cat is very distressed or is difficult to handle or restrain. He usually shaves a foreleg to identify where the relevant vein is situated, then injects a concentrated solution of anesthetic into that vein. The cat almost immediately goes to sleep. His breathing swiftly ceases, and then his heart stops beating.

In some cases, if the cat is very thin or the circulatory system isn't working efficiently, the necessary vein on the foreleg is not easy to find. When this occurs, the vet may need to inject directly into the heart or kidneys. Owners can find this distressing and be unable to hold their pet and keep him calm, so this is where the experienced handling and sympathetic soothing of a veterinary nurse can prove beneficial.

Afterward

If you wish, the vet will dispose of the body, arranging to have it buried or cremated on your instructions. Alternatively, you can take your cat home to bury him in a favorite area of the yard, if this is allowed. Graves should be at least 3 feet 3 inches (1 meter) deep and well away from water courses (your local environmental agency should able to advise you). Pet cemeteries and crematoriums will advise you on the costs and what is involved.

Frequently asked question

Q I am getting on in years and am worried about what will happen to my cat if I die before he does. How can I make sure my feline friend will be well cared for when I am gone?

A This is a very real worry for caring senior owners who may not be in the best of health or know they are quite likely to die before their pet does. If no relatives are willing to give the cat a good permanent home, some animal organizations will take on this responsibility and find the cat a home of which his old owner would have approved. To be sure that this happens in the event of death, the owner (or representative) should contact a group that makes such provisions to find out what to do beforehand, so that when the time comes, the cat can be transferred to the shelter or new home with a minimum of fuss and stress.

Grief

Only the owner can understand how it feels to lose a pet who meant the whole world to them, and it's important to realize that grieving is an essential part of the healing process after bereavement. There is no set time limit for how long owners should grieve; some are able to accept and recover from the loss more easily than others, who may not get over it for months or even years, and this is perfectly normal. However long it takes, don't be afraid to grieve when you feel the need to; bottling up grief inside you is bound to affect your own mental and physical health.

Help when you need it most

Sometimes you may feel that you are over the loss, but then grief hits you again at unexpected moments—such as when something triggers memories of your pet—and feelings of extreme sadness engulf you all over again. Again, this is normal. However, don't be afraid to lean on supportive family and friends when you feel the need, and do make use of the many excellent pet bereavement counseling services that are available by phone, letter, and e-mail; many animal organizations provide such a service, as do some pet insurance companies.

If overwhelming sorrow persists longer than you feel able to cope with, see an understanding doctor (but not necessarily your own if you don't feel comfortable doing so or you find she is not sympathetic and helpful). It may be that you need additional counseling or even medication to help ease debilitating grief and allow you to function with some normality again. Just talking to a sympathetic and understanding trained bereavement counselor can help you come to terms with your loss.

Physically marking your cat's passing with a grave and monument of some kind, whether a headstone, tree, shrub, or plant, to show where he lies and who he was, can prove therapeutic. You have somewhere tangible to go to mourn your pet and something to remember him by with gladness when the raw grief subsides.

For an elderly person, or one with limited time available, a more mature cat may be easier to accommodate than a kitten or active younger cat.

Everyone, even other pets, needs time to grieve before new pets are introduced to the household.

Children's reactions

Depending on their age, children react differently to the death of a pet. For many, it will be the first time they experience this inevitable part of life. This being the case, it will help enormously for a parent to talk things through with a bereavement counselor as to how to approach and explain pet death. The child may also find such supportive third-party help invaluable.

Never underestimate children's grief or reaction to the death of a pet, since it can affect them in many different ways that can have long-lasting and detrimental effects on their behavior, health, learning ability, and socialization. One thing you should *not* do is say that the pet was "put to sleep," since this can create false hope; the child may think that one day their pet friend will wake up and come back again.

Whether a child should be allowed to see the body of the pet depends on the age and personality of the child. A qualified counselor will be able to advise on the best course of action to take.

Pet grief

It's not just the owner who grieves over the loss of a pet; so can other animals in the household. Some people prefer to let the other animals see the body of their friend so they recognize that he has died and can say "goodbye." The best thing to do is continue with the remaining pets' routine as usual and let them work out a new hierarchy among themselves. Perhaps the last thing you need right now are the potential problems that introducing a new pet into the equation may well bring.

Top tip

After the death of a cat, don't get another one just because you think it will be beneficial to surviving pet(s). Although in some cases this has proved a success, sometimes they resent an intruder. If you do get another cat, wait until you feel emotionally and physically ready to cope with a new addition to the household (see pages 76–79 and 82–83).

Time for a successor

Only you will know when the time is right to get another cat. When it is, remember that there are plenty of homeless felines, young and old, waiting in animal shelters to fill the gap in the life of a special someone who can offer them the life they deserve—a good, caring home and lots of love.

INDEX

ACKNOWLEDGMENTS

Photographic Acknowledgments in Source Order

Ardea 73 bottom/Jean-Paul Ferrero 10
Bruce Coleman Collection/Heral Lange 121 bottom left, 129/Kim Taylor 124
Corbis UK Ltd/Lynda Richardson 7 bottom left, 67 bottom
Frank Lane Picture Agency/David Dalton 18 top/Philip Perry 66 bottom/Walther Rohdich 142
Getty Images/Kathi Lamm 59 top right, 71/Maria Spann 57/Arthur Tilley 80
Octopus Publishing Group Limited 6 bottom right, 12 bottom right, 18 bottom, 41, 43 left, 114/Jane Burton 1, 2–3, 9, 12 top right, 20 top, 21 top right, 21 bottom right, 21 bottom center, 24, 30 left, 30 right, 30 center, 32 top, 34 top left, 34 top right, 34 bottom left, 35 top, 35 bottom, 36 top, 36 bottom, 38, 40 top, 40 center, 40 bottom, 42 left, 42 right, 42 center, 44, 48 top, 50 bottom right, 52 bottom, 53, 54, 56, 60 center, 63 top left, 66 top, 69 bottom, 77, 78 top, 78 bottom, 81 left, 91 bottom right, 91 bottom left, 93 top left, 93 top right, 98, 101, 102, 103 top left, 103 top right, 103 bottom right, 103 bottom left, 104, 107 top left, 107 top right, 107 bottom right, 107 bottom left, 108, 109, 112 top left, 112 top right, 112 bottom right, 112 bottom left, 113, 113 bottom, 115, 136 top right, 136 bottom right, 136 bottom left, 137 left, 137 center, 139, 140, 143, 145 top left, 145 bottom left, 149 right, 149 center 150 top, 151 top, 153 top, 153 bottom, 156/Stephen Conroy 43 right/Nick Goodall 117 top left/Steve Gorton 5 top left, 5 center left, 8, 11, 13 top right, 13 bottom right, 20 bottom, 22, 26, 27, 47, 48 bottom, 49, 50 top left, 52 top, 55, 58 top right, 58 bottom left, 59 top left, 59 bottom right, 59 bottom left, 60 bottom, 61 top left, 61 center left, 61 top right, 62 top left, 62 top right, 64, 65, 67 top right, 68 top left, 68 bottom right, 69 top, 70, 73 top, 74, 75, 76, 79, 81 right, 82, 83, 85 top, 85 bottom, 86 top, 87 top left, 87 bottom right, 87 bottom left, 88, 89 top left, 89 bottom right, 90 bottom right, 93 bottom left, 94, 100, 106, 111 bottom, 117 bottom right, 120 top right, 120 bottom right, 120 bottom left, 130, 132, 133, 172, 173 bottom, 181 top right, 181 bottom right, 181 bottom left, 183 top, 184 top, 184 bottom, 188/Rosie Hyde/Stonehenge Veterinary Hospital 135, 171/Peter Loughran 16 top right, 37, 39, 71 top, 145 top right, 150 bottom right, 175 top/Ray Moller 15 top, 16 bottom left, 17 bottom right, 19 top left, 60 center right, 61 center right, 61 bottom right, 63 center/Dick Polak 159/George Taylor 118
Marc Henrie 7 bottom right, 25, 46, 51, 134, 155 bottom right, 169 top, 170, 174, 176, 181 top left, 182
RSPCA Photolibrary/Angela Hampton 154 bottom right, 165 right, 168
Dr A H Sparkes 164
Warren Photographic/Jane Burton 4, 5 top, 5 top center, 5 bottom right, 5 bottom left, 5 bottom center, 6 top right, 6 bottom left, 7 top left, 7 top right, 12 bottom left, 13 top left, 13 bottom left, 14, 15 center, 15 bottom, 16 center, 16 bottom right, 17 bottom left, 19 bottom, 23, 28, 29, 32 bottom, 33, 60, 60 top, 60 top left, 62 center, 62 bottom left, 63 bottom right, 84, 90 top left, 90 top right, 90 bottom left, 92, 96, 97, 99, 99 top right, 105, 110, 111 top, 116, 121 top left, 121 top right, 121 bottom right, 123, 125, 131, 136 top left, 137, 144 top, 144 bottom right, 144 bottom left, 145 bottom right, 146 top left, 146 center left, 146 top right, 146 center right, 146 bottom, 147 top left, 147 center left, 147 top right, 147 bottom, 148, 148 left, 148 right, 148 center left, 148 center right, 149 left, 151 bottom, 152, 154 top, 154 bottom left, 155 top left, 155 top right, 155 bottom left, 157, 158, 160, 161, 162, 165 left, 166, 167, 169, 175 bottom, 177, 179, 180 top, 180 bottom right, 180 bottom left, 183 bottom, 185, 186, 189